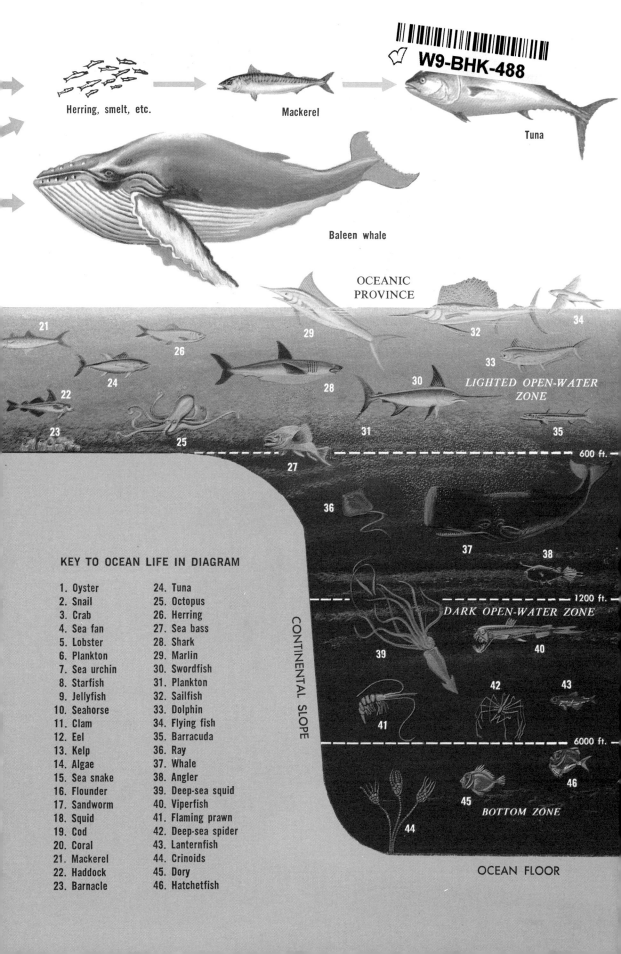

Herring, smelt, etc.

Mackerel

Tuna

W9-BHK-488

Baleen whale

OCEANIC PROVINCE

LIGHTED OPEN-WATER ZONE

600 ft.

DARK OPEN-WATER ZONE

1200 ft.

CONTINENTAL SLOPE

6000 ft.

BOTTOM ZONE

OCEAN FLOOR

KEY TO OCEAN LIFE IN DIAGRAM

1. Oyster	24. Tuna
2. Snail	25. Octopus
3. Crab	26. Herring
4. Sea fan	27. Sea bass
5. Lobster	28. Shark
6. Plankton	29. Marlin
7. Sea urchin	30. Swordfish
8. Starfish	31. Plankton
9. Jellyfish	32. Sailfish
10. Seahorse	33. Dolphin
11. Clam	34. Flying fish
12. Eel	35. Barracuda
13. Kelp	36. Ray
14. Algae	37. Whale
15. Sea snake	38. Angler
16. Flounder	39. Deep-sea squid
17. Sandworm	40. Viperfish
18. Squid	41. Flaming prawn
19. Cod	42. Deep-sea spider
20. Coral	43. Lanternfish
21. Mackerel	44. Crinoids
22. Haddock	45. Dory
23. Barnacle	46. Hatchetfish

PIONEERS OF OCEANOGRAPHY

by

DONALD W. COX, Ed.D.

portrait illustrations by
JACK WOODSON

Explorers of the Deep

INCORPORATED
MAPLEWOOD, NEW JERSEY

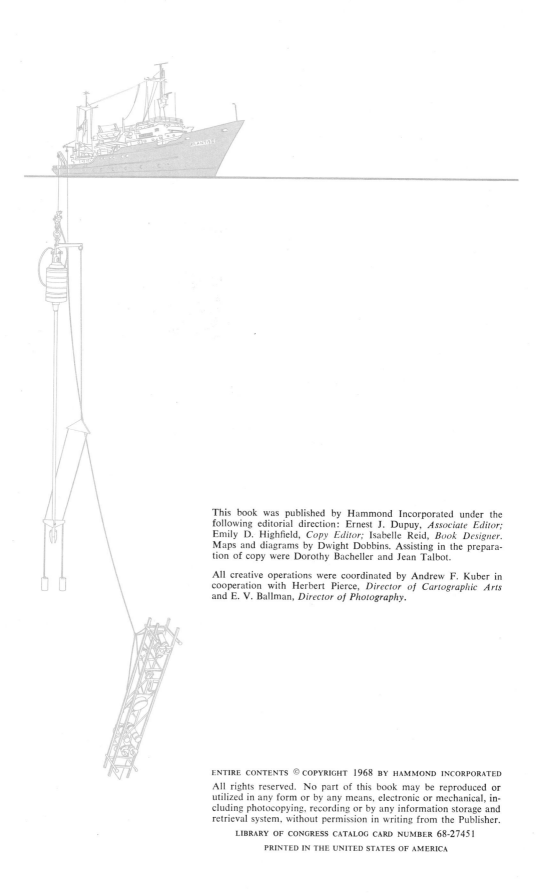

This book was published by Hammond Incorporated under the following editorial direction: Ernest J. Dupuy, *Associate Editor;* Emily D. Highfield, *Copy Editor;* Isabelle Reid, *Book Designer.* Maps and diagrams by Dwight Dobbins. Assisting in the preparation of copy were Dorothy Bacheller and Jean Talbot.

All creative operations were coordinated by Andrew F. Kuber in cooperation with Herbert Pierce, *Director of Cartographic Arts* and E. V. Ballman, *Director of Photography.*

Contents

Introduction

In the past two decades, more progress has been made in the exploration of the mysterious and largely uncharted realm that lies beneath the oceans than was made during thousands of years previous. This book attempts to show the great strides that have taken place in this new and exciting field through the stories of the lives of the new breed of ocean explorers and inventors who have made these advances possible. All of the 18 pioneers who are profiled have *one* characteristic in common: each was a maverick who took an independent course and challenged the established system of the times. All of them ran counter to the old way of doing things and yet were able to establish a creditable record of accomplishments despite leaving some chafened associates and bruised reputations in their wake.

The selection of personalities who were to be profiled in this volume has been a difficult one. My criteria of choice were based on a variety of personal reasons. Space limitations necessitated omitting many worthy candidates. Some of those prominent names which might otherwise have warranted inclusion are listed herewith.

In telling the story of the leading American oceanographers a special tribute should be paid first to Professor Alexander Dallas Bache, the almost forgotten grandson of Benjamin Franklin, who was the first person to carry out a systematic exploration of the Gulf Stream in the early 19th century, the charting of which his grandfather began in 1769.

Nor can one forget the contributions of Dr. George F. Bass, the youthful assistant professor of classical archaeology at the University of Pennsylvania. He is another little known name in the field, who has pioneered the search for artifacts from pre-Christian era shipwrecks found under the Mediterranean and Aegean Seas with the aid of his two-man submarine, *Asherah*.

Dr Eugenie Clark, the Director of the Cape Haze Marine Laboratory at Siesta Key, Sarasota, Florida, is a prominent distaff member of the present group of outstanding oceanographers. As a leading world authority on the behavior of sharks, triggerfish and the porcupine fish, she maintains a well-stocked lab and has made research dives in the Red Sea, Pacific Ocean, Gulf of Mexico and the Caribbean.

Two of these three names represent only a sampling of some of the more prominent and colorful American oceanographers, who currently are working on the wet frontier. They are sometimes also called aquanauts or oceanauts—terms which have become popular expressions to define these professional people who are experts in one or more of the marine sciences.

Oceanography as an organized science really had its beginnings almost a century ago with the *HMS Challenger*'s four-year cruise (1872-1876). Wyville Thomson, the director of the British *Challenger* expedition, set out to "learn everything about the sea." He included on his staff botanists, zoologists and chemists who, in turn, became specialists in their own field of marine science.

Despite its promising 19th-century beginnings, the 20th-century growth of this new science has been agonizingly slow. Although public and private oceanographic institutions for biological and general ocean research have proliferated in recent years, they have lacked the facilities and funds needed to carry out broad investigations of the seas. Marine research requires not only special ships and trained oceanographers and crews to man them but also shore-based laboratories, computers, and other expensive support equipment.

Now, thanks to recent events, the picture is changing and large grants of money for oceanographic research are finally becoming available. The sea is luring us back to her bosom. Over a century ago, Horace Greeley, the New York newspaper editor, coined an apt slogan: "Go West Young Man!" The slogan was fitting for the times since it paralleled America's push to the Pacific. A similar slogan for the present times which would be appropriate for the coming exploration and exploitation of the seas might be: "Get Wet Young Man!"

One of those who is preaching this slogan is Dr. Harris Stewart, the new Director of the U.S. Institute of Oceanography. He found himself playing the role of proselytizer for finding future marine scientists while on the International Indian Ocean Expedition in 1964. When the Coast and Geodetic Survey ship, *Pioneer,* steamed out of San Francisco on a six-month oceanographic voyage, Dr. Stewart was aboard as chief scientist. At each major port special two-day scientific seminars and open houses were held on shipboard for local scientists and curious citizens interested in the co-operative purposes of the expedition. Dr. Stewart commented on this diplomatic side effect: " . . . I think this was one aspect of the expedition that in the past ships have not concentrated on very much—this letting the people in the areas where our ships are working know why we are there and what we are doing and take them along with us to work . . . so that the work we are doing does not just come back to the United States but filters out to the other countries and perhaps helps them in their fisheries problem, their meteorological problems and their basic scientific problems."

One of the visitors to take advantage of the *Pioneer*'s open-ship policy when it stopped at Manila in the Philippine Islands was a young high school girl, Theresa Yang. In a poignant letter to Dr. Stewart, the officers and crew of the *Pioneer,* Miss Yang wrote:

Dear Sirs:
In behalf of my friends, I sincerely wish to thank you for your kindness in allowing us to tour your ship. If you only knew how much we enjoyed and profited from this. We honestly believe that you are the kindest and most patient foreigners we've ever met.

I know that we were a bunch of giggling, immature adolescents causing much trouble for poor Mr. Sweat. We do apologize and hope that the next time you come, you would see us a bit more grown up.

There were many of us who went there quite ignorant. We had heard of oceanography and we mistakenly thought of it as inferior to solar physics, biology, etc. I mean what is so important about the old sea? We thought that it was a dull, unadventurous job—sort of like taking a white collar job. But we know now that it is not. I know that Dr. Stewart would be very glad to hear this—I overheard one of the boys telling another that you have convinced him about oceanography and that he might study that for college. We may not all turn out to be oceanographers but you have planted in us that desire to search, to be curious, and the desire to learn.

So despite all the trouble we've caused you, I hope that this might make you feel good.

Yours sincerely,
Theresa Yang

Miss Yang's "desire to search . . . and learn" is the same as that held by older "searchers of the sea" who have responded to the seas' magnetic pull and whose achievements are narrated here.

Deep-sea angler.

Benjamin Franklin

Benjamin Franklin's intense scientific curiosity is well-known from his famous kite experiment and his astute theories on electricity. Thus, it should not be too surprising for us to learn that this landsman-scientist was equally involved in unraveling the mysteries of the sea even though oceanography as a science was yet unborn. According to his biographer, Carl Van Doren, Franklin showed his scientific bent and interest in the sea at the age of 20 by recording all that he saw on the return voyage from his first trip to England. In 1743, while serving as a member of the American Philosophical Society (our leading scientific institution of the time) he made an observation which ranks him with the first and best meteorologists. Franklin was a pioneer who foresaw the peculiar relationship of the weather to the sea. He had not forecast the weather annually — since 1732, as Poor Richard — for nothing.

"We were to have an eclipse of the moon at Philadelphia on a Friday evening in October about nine o'clock. I intended to observe it, but was prevented by a northeast storm which came on about seven with thick clouds, as usual, that quite obscured the whole hemisphere. . . . ." After checking with his brother in Boston by letter and discovering that the storm did not begin there until nearly 11 o'clock that same evening, he concluded:

"From thence I formed an idea of the cause of these storms, which I would explain by a familiar instance or two. Suppose a long canal of water stopped at the end by a gate. The water is quite at rest till the gate is open, then it begins to move out through the gate; the water next to the gate is first in motion, and moves toward the gate; the water next to the first water moves next, and so on successively until the water at the head of the canal is in motion, which is last of all. In this case all the water moves indeed towards the gate, but the successive times of beginning motion are the contrary way, viz., from the gate backwards to the head of the canal. Again, suppose the air in a chamber at rest, no current in the room till you make a fire in the chimney. Immediately the air in the chimney, being rarefied by the fire, rises; the air next to the chimney flows in to supply its place, moving towards the chimney; and in consequence the rest of the air successively, quite back to the door. Thus to produce our northeast storms I suppose some great heat and rarefaction of the air in or about the Gulf of Mexico; the air thence rising has its place supplied by the next northern, cooler, and therefore denser and heavier air, etc., etc., in a successive current, to which current our coast and inland ridge of mountains give the direction of northeast, as they lie northeast and southwest."

Franklin's incisive observation, made before the invention of the telephone, radio, Tiros and Nimbus weather satellites, meteorological balloons and other modern aids to the forecaster, marked a significant first prediction of things-to-come in the linkage of weather systems over land areas with their origins over the oceans.

This scientific interest in the causes of weather closely paralleled that of another developing Franklin curiosity — ocean currents and their peculiar behavior. Since the Atlantic Ocean had been crossed and recrossed for centuries since the time of Columbus, most seafaring men, in the days of sailing vessels, were familiar with the strongly running Equatorial Current. Many vessels intending to pass down into the South Atlantic found they could make no headway unless they made necessary tracks to the east in the region of the southeast trades. When Ponce de Leon's three ships left Cape Canaveral on the east coast of Florida for the Tortugas to the south in 1513, they found that at times they could not stem the Gulf Stream. "Although they had great wind," de Leon wrote, "they could not proceed forward but backward." A few years later, Spanish shipmasters learned to take advantage of the currents, sailing westward in the Equatorial Current, but returning home via the Gulf Stream as far as Cape Hatteras, whence they turned east out into the open Atlantic.

With the advent of regular open ocean voyages by sailing ships between the continents in the 17th and 18th centuries, navigators began to accumulate more and more knowledge about surface currents. Most old sailing records, however, show little that could be called scientific studies until Benjamin Franklin, that "wisest American," took a personal interest in the most famous Atlantic current separating the New World from the Old — the Gulf Stream.

When he was Deputy Postmaster of what were then the British Colonies in North America, Benjamin Franklin found himself in a perplexing dilemma. In 1769, the Board of Customs in Boston complained to him in Philadelphia that the mail packets coming from England took about two weeks longer to make the westward crossing than did the Rhode Island merchant ships. Franklin took the problem to a Nantucket sea captain, Timothy Folger, a cousin, who told him that the information might be true, because the Rhode Island captains were well acquainted with the peculiar characteristics of the Gulf Stream and avoided it on the westward crossing while the English captains did not.

Franklin related how Folger and other Nantucket whalers were personally familiar with the Gulf Stream and had tried to describe its peculiarities as a courtesy to the English captains.

". . . in our pursuit of whales, which keep to the sides of it but are not met within it, we run along the side and frequently cross it to change our side, and in crossing it have sometimes met and spoke with those packets who were in the middle of it and stemming it. We have informed them that they were stemming a current that was against them to the value of three miles an hour and advised them to cross it, but they were too wise to be counseled by simple American fisherman."

Franklin, thinking it was a pity no notice was taken of this current upon their charts, asked Folger to mark it out for him to the best of his ability.

Franklin was convinced that the Gulf Stream was worth studying. He dug down into his pocket to finance a study of its peculiarities, reckoning, rightly, that a good chart of the North Atlantic currents would improve the regularity of the mail-boat packet service between the two continents. The correct course of the Gulf Stream was duly plotted on an old chart of the Atlantic. This chart, with Folger's sailing directions, was then sent by Franklin to Falmouth, England, for use by captains of the packets. Unfortunately, the results of his efforts, which marked the beginning of oceanographic research in America, were ignored by the stubborn English sea captains who didn't like being told anything about navigation by an upstart colonist.

In the spring of 1775 Franklin was in England trying to prevent open hostilities between the Colonies and their mother country. His efforts were to no avail, and he embarked for Philadelphia with his young grandson, Temple. The tranquil six-week voyage belied the storm clouds which were threatening outside garrisoned Boston. Franklin wrote, "The weather was constantly so moderate that a London wherry might have accompanied us all the way." On the second half of the voyage, he began to take daily temperature readings of the air and water and to study the Gulf Stream which had interested him six years earlier. During the week of April 26 to May 2, 1775, he lowered his thermometer into the ocean from two-to four-times a day from as early as seven in the morning to as late as eleven at night, while the ship kept along the edge of the Gulf Stream and then cut across it into colder water. He had seen a whale on the 26th before they

entered but had seen none in the actual stream itself.

He noticed that the water in the stream had its own color and more gulfweed than the surrounding water, and that "it does not sparkle in the night." It might be studied and understood like a river, he surmised. "A vessel from Europe to North America may shorten her passage by avoiding to stem the stream, in which the thermometer will be very useful; and a vessel from America to Europe may do the same by the same means by keeping in it. It may have often happened accidentally that voyages have been shortened by these circumstances. It is well to have command of them."

When he arrived at Philadelphia on May 5th, he heard of the bloody outbreaks at Lexington and Concord and the next morning he was chosen by the Assembly to be one of its deputies to the Second Continental Congress. The Revolutionary War and its aftermath forced him to curtail his scientific research for the next decade.

In late July 1785, Franklin began his eighth and last voyage to America from Europe. It was probably the most cheerful of all his journeys back to the New World. The 79-year-old man believed that his public life was at last over and that he could now devote his remaining years to science. On the second day out, he began his daily observation records of the temperature of the air and water with the help of Jonathan Williams. On August 14th and September 11th, they tried to determine the temperature of the water at 18 and 20 fathoms by letting down a bottle and a keg. Still as much interested in the Gulf Stream as ever, Franklin continued to take notes on the color of the current and the presence of the gulfweed. He wrote more on scientific matters during that August on shipboard than in any other month of his entire life. In a long letter to a friend, Julien-David LeRoy, the aged man jotted down what he called his *Maritime Observations.*

Benjamin Franklin's famous chart of the Gulf Stream as it appeared in the printing of 1786.

In that comprehensive scientific survey, Franklin covered such important contributions to ship safety as a device to keep hawsers from breaking at the sudden swell of a wave; the use of watertight compartments in a ship to prevent sinking; fire fighting; collision with other ships or icebergs; the construction and operation of Eskimo kayaks and Indian canoes; paddlewheels to serve as auxiliaries to the wind; swimming anchors to retard the motion of vessels during gales in water too deep for anchorage; the Gulf Stream's cause and uses; suggestions for the management of lifeboats; escape from wrecks; and improved diets for sailors.

Once Franklin intended to stop his letter, but confessed: "The garrulity of an old man has got hold of me, and, as I may never have another occasion of writing on this subject, I think I may as well now, once and for all, empty my nautical budget." He continued in encyclopedic high spirits and ended with a satirical paragraph on the evil uses of navigation in transporting useless luxuries and carrying on the cruel slave trade.

Franklin saw to it that his Gulf Stream chart was eventually published in the *Transactions of the American Philosophical Society* in 1786. The thriftiness of the Philosophical Society editors in saving paper and printing costs led them to combine on one plate Franklin's now famous Gulf Stream chart with a wholly separate figure intended to illustrate a research paper by John Gilpin on the "Annual Migrations of the Herring."

Present day oceanographers have modified Franklin's findings somewhat. They speak of the Gulf Stream System, reflecting the discovery that east of Cape Hatteras there is no longer a continuous river of warm water but a "series of overlapping currents arranged somewhat like the shingles on a roof." Not only do the streams "overlap" but they also wander about from time to time and create side currents.

Modern men of science with their research aids and equipment may continue to modify or even discard Franklin's early findings but few can match the alertness and enthusiasm of that early searcher of the sea.

Charles Wilkes

A little-known naval hero, who rose to the rank of admiral despite two court-martials, became the first American mariner after Franklin to take an interest in unraveling the mysteries of the sea. Lt. Charles Wilkes was his name, and although he did not achieve the fame of other 19th century American naval heroes like Jones, Perry, Farragut or Dewey, he headed the greatest—albeit least known—naval expedition ever launched by this country.

Wilkes was born in New York City on April 3, 1798, the son of John Wilkes, a successful businessman and nephew of a prominent British politician. His father gave young Charles a good preliminary education in mathematics, navigation, drawing and foreign languages.

He entered the infant Merchant Marine in 1815 and three years later became a midshipman in the United States Navy. After attending the naval school in Boston (Annapolis had not yet opened), he was ordered to sea duty. He served first in the Mediterranean aboard the *Guerriere* and then in the Pacific on the *Franklin*. During the long periods between sailing orders, young Wilkes studied under Ferdinand Hassler, the founder of the U.S. Coast and Geodetic Survey.

After completing a two-year survey of Narragansett Bay in Rhode Island, he was designated in 1833 to head a new Navy unit, the Depot of Charts and Instruments, forerunner of the present Naval Oceanographic Office. The Navy had established the Depot in 1830 to collect, care for, and issue charts and navigational instruments for its ships. In the past, the Navy had been forced to rely primarily on foreign charts which were unsatisfactory from the standpoint of language and uniformity. Charts obtained from commercial sources were generally unreliable. The Depot acquired a lithographic press and began printing its own nautical charts. Wilkes volunteered to survey and chart several bodies of water adjacent to North America and completed a hydrographic survey of Georges Bank.

A more ambitious undertaking, however, was already under way. For over a decade Congress had been deliberating the merits of an exploring and charting expedition to the Pacific Ocean and the South Seas. The idea, first aired in 1810, had the support of former President John Quincy Adams who had tried to launch such an effort during his administration. By 1836 complaints of shipowners and whalers concerning the dangers to navigation in the poorly charted Pacific had reached a point where Congress could no longer delay. In May of that year Congress voted $300,000 for the expedition.

From the very beginning the "United States Exploring Expedition," as it was designated, was beset by controversy and delay. Two years passed with no visible progress by the Navy in launching the expedition. President Martin Van Buren intervened, and called for a new commander of the expedition. Although only a junior officer, Lt. Wilkes was selected after several higher ranking officers had declined and others had been passed over.

Wilkes plunged ahead in his new role and completed the organization of the expedition within five months' time. Besides obtaining the necessary naval complement of surveyors, etc., he rounded up a civilian corps of scientists which included James D. Dana, mineralogist, and Charles Pickering, zoologist. The intent was to gather meteorological, botanical, geo-logical and even philological data in the areas explored.

The squadron of six ships commanded by Wilkes consisted of the 780-ton sloop of war, *Vincennes,* which served as flagship; the *Peacock,* a 650-ton sloop of war; the 230-ton brig, *Porpoise;* two small New York pilot boats renamed the *Sea Gull* and the *Flying Fish*; and the supply ship, *Relief.*

Wilkes ended up with only four ships for most of the expedition. The *Sea Gull* was lost with all hands during a storm off Cape Horn. The *Relief* was found to be too slow a sailer and was sent home after landing stores in Hawaii and Australia. The *Peacock* was wrecked while entering the mouth of the Columbia River and was replaced by the *Oregon.*

The squadron sailed from Norfolk, Virginia, on August 8, 1838. It rounded Cape Horn after several stops in the Atlantic and made its first penetration of polar waters near Captain Cook's "farthest south" in early 1839. After a rendezvous at Valparaíso and a stop at Callao, the expedition proceeded to the Tuamotu, Society and Samoan Islands. While the hydrographic teams proceeded with methodical surveying plans devised by Wilkes, the nine-man scientific corps began their work of collecting specimens and recording scientific and cultural data.

From Sydney, Australia, the squadron next sailed south through ever colder waters until polar pack ice was reached on January 11, 1840. Five days later the elusive southern continent was sighted. Despite the hazards of ice which had already damaged two of the ships, Wilkes pressed on to explore the coast from 160° East longitude to 100° East, a distance of about 1,500 miles. He had changed hundreds of years of speculation by demonstrating the existence of the huge continent which he named Antarctica. Today that portion explored by the *Vincennes* and *Porpoise* is named Wilkes Land in his honor.

Following the Antarctic cruise he returned to the survey of the islands in the southwest Pacific. During the visit to the Fiji Islands Wilkes' nephew and another crew member were clubbed to death by native savages. The squadron next headed for the Hawaiian Islands for refitting and a well-earned rest. Wilkes personally saw to the setting up of an observation post on the volcano, Mauna Loa.

In May 1841, Wilkes again touched the North American continent when he entered the Strait of Juan de Fuca near Vancouver, Canada. Surveys were made along the coast for 800 miles and exploration parties journeyed far inland. These surveys in the Northwest were particularly important and timely for the United States in view of the then current dispute with Britain over the Oregon country. In November of the same year the expedition returned to Hawaii and thence to the Philippines. After a stop at Singapore, where the *Flying Fish* was sold, the expedition set sail for home via the Cape of Good Hope. Two of the remaining three vessels which reached New York on June 9, 1842 had sailed 90,000 miles.

During the course of the expedition Wilkes conducted 234 hydrographic surveys and determined over 2,000 geographical positions by astronomical and trigonometric means. Some 280 islands in the Pacific Ocean were mapped and the position of many of them was accurately fixed for the first time.

Over 500 drawings of headlands and entrances to harbors had been made. Endless data and specimens in the fields of marine biology, meteorology, geology, zoology—through the whole spectrum of sciences — had been accumulated by the scientific corps attached to the expedition.

Once the four-year epic voyage was over, instead of recognition for his efforts, Wilkes found himself condemned for alleged cruelty to his crewmen. His tough, driving manner and quick temper had won him few friends, either in Washington or at sea. He was a strict disciplinarian when it came to meting out punishment to disorderly crew members and sometimes ordered forty-one lashes instead of the prescribed twelve. This charge was used against him in a court-martial and served to keep him from the promotions he deserved. From 1843 to 1861 Wilkes remained on special duty preparing the reports of the expedition.

The official story of the ocean cruise was written by Wilkes under the title: *Narrative of the United States Exploring Expedition.* Its five volumes and atlas took two years to publish. Although the original publication of the *Narrative* was limited by law to an official edition of only one hundred copies, the resulting clamor for his work led to the printing of several unofficial editions running into thousands of copies. Twenty-two scientific volumes and twelve atlases were also published over the years under the editorship of Wilkes. He, himself, was the author of the special volumes, *Meteorology* and *Hydrography*. The beautifully illustrated volumes in the science series dealt with such subjects as crustaceans, sponges and corals, sea-bed formations, and the races of man.

Work on this massive project was interrupted by the outbreak of the Civil War. Wilkes was given command of the cruiser, *San Jacinto* to search for the Confederate commerce destroyer, *Sumter*. On the 8th of November 1861, Wilkes stopped the British mail ship, *Trent*, and removed two representatives of the Confederacy, John Slidell and James Mason, who were on their way to Europe to ask aid from England and France for the Southern cause. Wilkes' high-handed action almost precipitated the involvment of the Union in a war with England.

Although Wilkes was hailed as a hero in the North for forcibly removing Mason and Slidell from the ship, the United States

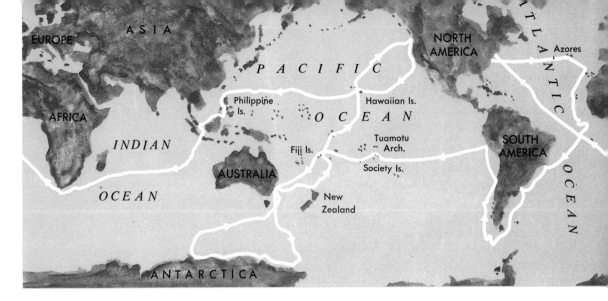

Generalized track of the United States Exploring Expedition commanded by Charles Wilkes.

did not have a good case since it had violated British neutrality. President Lincoln disavowed the action and the two Confederate commissioners were soon released.

In 1862, despite his impetuousness, Wilkes was promoted to the rank of Commodore and put in charge of a flying squadron operating against blockade runners in the West Indies. Although he failed to capture any Confederate ships, he managed to offend several foreign governments through his continuing brash acts, which led to his recall by Secretary Welles on June 1, 1863.

In 1864, his collision course with Navy superiors earned him his second court-martial, and he was found guilty of "insubordination and conduct unbecoming of an officer," for which he was given a public reprimand and suspended from duty for three years. The period of suspension was later reduced to one year.

Following his retirement in 1866, he was advanced to the rank of Rear Admiral as a reward for his earlier services. His retirement gave him an opportunity to take up the editing of the still unfinished reports of the U.S. Exploring Expedition. Fortunately for Wilkes, Congress had repeatedly appropriated the necessary funds to continue the work. Besides the published twenty-two scientific volumes, an additional three volumes were prepared but never printed. He did much of his work in the famous Dolley Madison House in Washington where he lived in his last years, concluding his part in the monumental task three years before his death in 1877.

Wilkes' achievements earned him wide recognition, especially abroad, where he received the Founder's Gold Medal of the Royal Geographic Society of England for his discoveries and accounts. Both the *Narrative* and the scientific volumes of the expedition rate as classics of scientific exploration. Scientist-expedition members, such as Dana and Pickering, built international and lasting reputations with their published reports.

The hydrographic charts alone were a major accomplishment and worth the full cost of the expedition. Original prints of the 106 charts prepared by Wilkes are now scarce collectors' items. For decades, however, they were the mainstay of our nautical knowledge of the Pacific. As late as World War II the U.S. Navy depended on Wilkes' Pacific charts for invasion plans of famous isles such as Tarawa. Taken as a group, these charts tell the story of the first great coordinated effort in marine exploration. The track of the last big circumnavigational expedition depending solely on sail reflected the scientific coming of age of a young nation and the beginnings of a new science—oceanography.

Matthew Fontaine Maury

In August 1825, midshipman Matthew Fontaine Maury reported for Naval training aboard his first ship, the naval frigate *Brandywine* in New York. This vessel had been assigned the honor of taking Lafayette home to France for the last time. The young Maury was partly disappointed in the voyage because of the lack of educational facilities offered aboard ship. He wanted to learn navigation but discovered that the only textbook in the ship's library was in Spanish. In his free time he waded through this text with the aid of a Spanish dictionary. Maury also used his time while on watch to learn spherical geometry by sketching problems on the cannonballs in their racks.

Late one afternoon, while repeating his theorems, young Maury heard a voice behind him say, "So, the cannonball has gone to school." Looking up, he saw the white-haired Lafayette standing behind him. Overcome with embarrassment, he stammered, "I expect, sir, you wonder why. It seemed easier to understand on a sphere." Then Lafayette quickly replied, "No my young friend, I never ask why. Only why not? CUR NON is my motto. When I came to America a long time ago to help a new nation fight for a new kind of freedom, my friends asked me, Why? I answered CUR NON." The old general's voice deepened and his eyes flashed. "Then it was nothing but an idea. But an idea worth fighting for."

Bursting with pride that the noble Frenchman had noticed him, Maury blurted out, "I guess there is nothing more powerful than an idea. If you believe in it enough, it is worth fighting for. CUR NON will be my motto too." Lafayette gave the boy a pat on the back as Maury went back to studying his cannonball.

Maury, born near Fredericksburg, Virginia on January 4, 1806 and educated at Harpeth Academy, was appointed a midshipman in the U.S. Navy at the age of 19. The fact that his brother had died of yellow fever while serving in the Navy did not daunt Matthew.

As an officer of the Navy, Maury had made several extensive voyages and had become known as an expert on navigation when in 1839 the turning point of his life occurred. At age 33, in the prime of life, he suffered a grievous stagecoach accident near Fredericksburg. He had given up his seat and was riding with the coachman when the wagon overturned. His thighbone was broken and a knee dislocated. The bones did not knit properly and after a painful convalescence he was rendered permanently lame. Fortunately the Navy did not forcibly retire him.

While recuperating from his accident Maury became irritated with his enforced idleness. Under the pseudonym of Henry Bluff, he wrote some articles criticizing the Navy. These were published in the *Southern Literary Messenger*. He took the Navy to task for its lack of an academy for training future officers, its unpreparedness for war, the need for hydrographic study of the West Coast, the need for support of commerce with China, and for the protection of American fishermen on whaling grounds. (His dream of a Naval Academy became a reality in 1845 and Maury was later to be dubbed the "Father of Annapolis.")

In 1842 the Navy was reorganized along the lines of the present bureau system and the Depot of Charts and Instruments was placed under the then Bureau of Ordnance and Hydrography. Congress authorized the construction of a new building for the Depot and assigned lame Lt. Maury as Officer-in-Charge.

Maury had set an ambitious program for himself as head of the Depot, for the rigors and uncertainties of life at sea had made him acutely aware of the potential value of charts showing the average direction and strength of winds and currents. He described his goal in life as "nothing less than to blaze a way through the winds of the sea by which the navigator may find the best paths at all seasons."

Some years earlier he had published a treatise on navigation in which he postulated the need for the systematic collection of data about the winds and ocean currents. He now saw that if enough weather and sea information were available, charts and sailing directions could be compiled indicating the most favorable routes for sailing vessels. Maury proceeded to work out a plan of collecting data supplied by ships at sea. The first step required the cooperation of dozens of commercial and military ships' captains scattered all over the globe.

He invited officers of outbound ships to record ten categories of hydrographic information in special log forms made up by Maury. The logs were to be returned to him for evaluation. Mariners were asked to throw tightly corked bottles which Maury called "mute little navigators," into the water to help prepare estimates of the speed and direction of the ocean currents. Most ships' masters fussed and fumed at this request stating, "It's just a fool scheme of some crackpot in Washington." They refused to take any readings or to complete the reporting forms distributed by Maury. A whole year passed before a single record was returned. But Maury was patient. He could wait.

In the meantime, Maury also began collecting meteorological and oceanographic data from old logs of men-of-war and merchant vessels from other nations besides the United States. He added their reports on winds, currents and water temperatures to those returned by American whalers and other ships cruising the oceans.

George Bancroft, the new Secretary of the Navy under President Polk, was favorably impressed with the possibilities of the charts and he invited Maury to read a paper explaining them before the National Institute. Bancroft also ordered all ships of the Navy to keep special log books, devised by Maury, for recording observations on conditions at sea.

Depot of Charts and Instruments (later the Naval Observatory and Hydrographic Office).

As the information needed by Maury began to come in, the painstaking job of preparing charts from this mass of data got under way. In 1848 the first wind and current charts and sailing directions were published. Once shipowners and captains began to use them the sailing time between points was appreciably shortened. The passage to Rio de Janeiro from the eastern United States was cut by ten days. The long trip from New York around Cape Horn to California was cut from six to five months, a welcome saving of time.

The success of the charts, in turn, motivated the calling of an international marine conference which was held at Brussels in 1853 to investigate the possibilities of devising a cooperative and uniform system of meteorological observations at sea. Maury played a leading role in the conference and would have thrown it open to the consideration of land as well as ocean weather observation. Others, however, wanted to restrict it to the sea. Nevertheless, Maury is credited with inspiring the establishment of the official meteorological offices in both Great Britain and Germany. Other maritime nations at this conference, taking a cue from the demonstrated value of Maury's charts, began establishing their own hydrographical services which often cooperated with one another and with Maury in charting the seas. The Brussels conference marked the starting point of the international science of physical oceanography and, through Maury's energy and initiative, a worldwide cooperative system was organized using Maury's standard reporting forms.

Maury summed up his early achievement with this remark: "Every ship that navigates the high seas with these charts and blank abstract logs on board may henceforth be regarded as a floating laboratory, a temple of science." Recognition came to him from many sources, including honorary degrees from several universities, but the Navy did not reward him with any advancement in rank.

Maury's interest in the science of the sea was not restricted to surface wind and current investigations. He persuaded the Navy to let him combine the chart work with bottom soundings. Sounding lines were used to bring up samples from the bottom. But too often the weighted hemp sounding lines would break until a young midshipman, John Brooke, came to Maury with a solution: place a sounding weight (actually a cannonball) in a small soap-lined cup with a hollow tube attached. After the ball has driven the tube into the seabed, the ball is released and the tube with its sample of bottom-deposit reeled in. The system worked beautifully but the soft yellow clay brought up from the first deep-sea soundings looked disappointing until Maury sent it to his friend, Professor Bailey, a famous microscopist at West Point. Bailey was delighted when he discovered that imbedded in the material were the shells of dead microscopic marine animals that proved to be valuable guides in the just beginning studies of life in the sea.

By 1854 (the year the Navy changed the name of Maury's office to the Naval Observatory and Hydrographical Office) Maury had collected a number of deep water soundings. This early work provided the foundation for Maury's active role in obtaining exact information about the Atlantic seabed for the laying of the underwater cable linking America and Europe. What had seemed like scientific foolishness now assumed an unlooked-for role of practical importance.

Maury's great work, *The Physical Geography of the Sea,* published in 1855, can be regarded as a milestone in the development of the new science of oceanography. It is a lasting monument to the author. This important book which treated, for the first time, the whole structure of the sea was so popular that it ran into nineteen editions and was translated into a half-dozen foreign languages. Maury revised the book several times, adding and rejecting material with the remark: "I am wedded to no theories and do not advocate the doctrines of any particular school. Truth is my objective."

Wind and current maps of the world were possible only after the systematic collection of data.

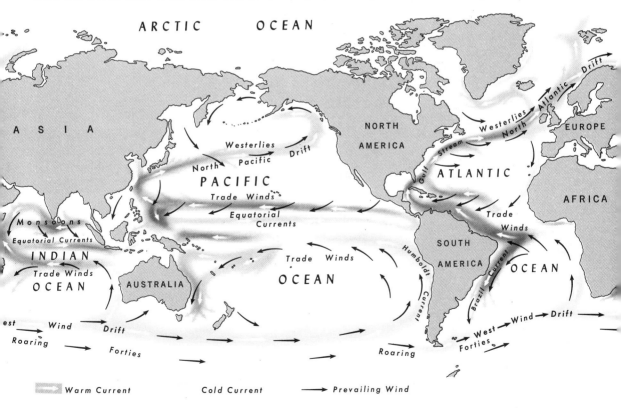

21

Like pioneer Benjamin Franklin before him Matthew Maury was mesmerized by the Gulf Stream and explained it in poetic terms in his book. "There is a river in the ocean. In the severest droughts it never fails, and in the mightiest floods it never overflows. Its banks and bottom are of cold water while its current is warm. The Gulf of Mexico is its fountain and its mouth is the Arctic Ocean. It is the Gulf Stream," wrote Maury in 1855. Maury would have welcomed the modern view of the Gulf Stream as a series of currents rather than a single flowing river since he was wedded to no one theory. He concluded his discussion of the Gulf Stream by saying: "In the present state of our knowledge concerning this wonderful phenomenon—for the Gulf Stream is one of the most marvelous things in the ocean—we can do little more than conjecture. But he who contemplates the sea must look upon it as a part of the exquisite machinery by which the harmonies of Nature are preserved."

In 1855, a Retirement Board established by an Act of Congress placed Maury on the retired list without a hearing of any kind. "Clearing out the dead wood," the Navy said, which aroused Maury's indignation. He insisted, despite this slight by the Navy, that "If I had to choose between being a commander or a captain and originating the Wind and Current Charts, I'd take the charts." After over two years of intercession by hundreds of his friends, including General Sam Houston, Maury was restored to active duty and raised to the rank of Commander in 1858.

With the advent of the Civil War, the flow of meteorological and hydrographic data sent to Washington from the world's merchant fleet temporarily ceased. Maury, who had been honored with a promotion to Admiral, cast his lot with the Confederacy, first in harbor defense and then as an agent in England. After the war, he served under Maximilian in Mexico (1865-66) where he attempted to establish colonies for ex-Confederates. Failing in this mission, he returned to the United States in 1868 and was named professor of meteorology at the Virginia Military Institute.

In the meantime, the Hydrographic Office had been reorganized along the lines originally proposed by Maury. The Office was separated from the Naval Observatory and its functions were expanded to include responsibility for providing charts, sailing directions, and manuals to be used by vessels of the United States, and for the benefit and use of navigators generally. Three years after the inception of the new Office, the first "Notice to Mariners" for updating charts was published and sales agents were authorized in several major ports.

Maury was not a true oceanographer in the modern sense. His major contribution was a practical one stemming from his deciphering and analyzing a jumble of marine observations taken at widely scattered times and places, and then issuing a meaningful picture of the average conditions of the oceans on the sea lanes of the world. In effect he established the world's first oceanic meteorological data center. Maury, however, was the first man to foresee the interrelationships of the winds, currents, chemicals and temperature. This view of the sea as a single dynamic entity led to his being looked on today as a founder of oceanography.

In his later years Maury was offered the presidency of half a dozen colleges. He turned them all down for he was a sad and broken man. After Maury died in 1873, the following inscription was placed on his monument:

> Matthew Fontaine Maury
> Pathfinder of the Sea
> The genius who first snatched
> From ocean and atmosphere
> The secrets of the sea.

Alexander Agassiz

In spite of sporadic interest shown by countries in pursuing the science of the seas during the mid-19th century, oceanography remained a young and struggling science as far as an organized research effort was concerned. Broad investigation of the seas was dependent on parallel advances in the basic sciences which are the foundation stones of oceanography—physics, biology, chemistry and geology, as well as development of a research technology. Oceanography finally came of age in the latter part of the 19th century from the impetus given it by the work of men in associated fields.

One such stimulus came from the biologists. The English naturalist Edward Forbes (1815-1854) questioned the possibility of animal and plant life below 300 fathoms, beginning a debate on how deep in the ocean life did exist. In 1859 the publication of Darwin's *On the Origin of Species* with its emphasis on the relationship between fossils and living forms brought to the search for life in the ancestral seas a new dimension—time.

In the 1870's country after country took up the challenge and sponsored worldwide ocean-going expeditions with charting ships outfitted with laboratories and dredging gear. In 1872, the British corvette *HMS Challenger* set out on a three and a half-year cruise to examine the physical and biological conditions of the great ocean basins. Leadership in the American effort in this assault on the seas went to a Swiss-American scientist and mining engineer, Alexander Agassiz. This son of the famed Harvard naturalist, Louis Agassiz, was an outstanding and perhaps the last representative of the now-considered classic period in oceanography.

23

Various forms of plankton, the microscopic plants and minute animals which are the first links in the great chain of life in the sea.

Among his contributions to the new marine science were: the first use of steel cables for deep-sea dredging in place of the short-lived rope hawsers; the most extensive soundings of the Caribbean, Indian and tropical Pacific Oceans made before or since; and the invention of several ingenious pieces of oceanographic equipment like the "Agassiz trawl" and a new type of towing net for collection of plankton from different levels. Sir John Murray, who sailed as a scientist on the *Challenger* expedition and edited the famous *"Challenger* Reports" even went so far as to say that the advanced state of oceanography at the time probably owed more to the work and inspiration of Alexander Agassiz than to any other single man.

Alexander was strongly influenced by his father, Louis Agassiz, a leading authority on both living and fossil fish. The pater familias had preceded his family to the New World in order to learn more about the natural history and geology of North America as well as to deliver a series of lectures. The elder Agassiz won respect in scientific circles and was offered a professorship of zoology at Harvard. When his wife died of tuberculosis in 1848, Louis decided to send for his three children, two daughters and a son. So when he was 13, young Alexander Agassiz left Switzerland to join his father.

After crossing the Atlantic, Alexander quickly learned English in Cambridge High School and entered Harvard at the age of 15. His well-trained mind made him the envy of his fellow students. He served as bow oar on the Harvard crew and played lead roles in university theatricals. Agassiz concentrated on chemistry, geology, mathematics and zoology, the latter being his favorite subject. To help supplement the tight family budget while he was attending college he taught classes in the school for girls that his stepmother set up in the busy Agassiz house.

Upon graduation from Harvard in 1855, he was warned by his father that it would be too difficult to make a living as a naturalist, so he enrolled at the nearby Lawrence Scientific School where he studied to become a mining engineer. Graduating magna cum laude, he set off for San Francisco as a surveyor's aid for the Coast Survey on the ship *Fauntleroy.* The task of the expedition was to chart the boundary between the United States and British Columbia in the waters of the Straits of Georgia and Juan de Fuca. When the fall fogs became so dense in the strait that it was impossible for the men to carry on their surveying, Alexander spent his time making a study of jellyfish and collecting a number of perch. He also sent sketches and descriptions of marine life on the seashore of the Northwest Coast to his father in Boston.

After a summer in the Coast Survey, followed by a three-month stint in Panama, Alexander decided that government service offered no more opportunity of making quick money than did his first love—the teaching of natural science. So he resigned from the Coast Survey and returned to his father's museum and his sweetheart, Anna Russel, whom he had met in his stepmother's school. He was soon appointed an agent for the Harvard Museum of Comparative Zoology at the munificent salary of $1,500 a year. This turn of "fortune" opened the doors for marriage and the opportunity to obtain another degree in zoology.

When the Civil War commenced, most of the employees of the museum left to join the Union Army, but Agassiz, who had just become an American citizen, decided not to take sides, but to remain behind and keep the museum alive. He became more involved in the study of marine animals and now added the dory and seaside laboratory to his researches which committed him to marine biology for the rest of his life.

Agassiz then wrote a series of papers on the embryology of sea urchins and starfish. In 1865, he and his stepmother published *Seashore Studies in Natural History* and a few years later *Marine Animals of Massachusetts Bay*, both of which were accurate and fascinating studies. But Alexander soon found that his salary was not enough to support a wife and three small sons so he started looking around for a better paying job.

In 1866 he took a leave of absence from the museum and undertook the task of running the Calumet and Hecla copper mines in northern Michigan. His efforts in getting the rundown mines operating at a profit were successful, although the arduous work and the climate almost ruined his health. By 1869 the mines no longer required his full-time direction and were earning him, as president, a substantial income. He, therefore, decided to return to his career as a naturalist. To regain his health and give him a chance to renew acquaintances Alexander and his family made an extended visit to Europe. While there, he met some of the great European scientists like Darwin, Thomas Huxley and Richard Owen. He was particularly impressed with Charles Wyville Thomson in Belfast, who told him of dredging animals off the bottom of the sea at an unbelievable depth of 2,500 fathoms. (Thomson was to lead the famous *Challenger* expedition the following year which was to revolutionize the infant science of oceanography.)

Alexander returned from Europe with renewed enthusiasm although he had not completely recovered his health. Then, in 1873, both his father and wife died within a week of each other, and Alexander was heartbroken. In his deep sorrow, he evolved a philosophy of life that he followed to the end: "To live our lives as they have been made for us, and live in hope, do the best we can, work hard, and have as many interests as possible in what is going on around us." In 1876, when the *Challenger* returned from her historic world cruise, Alexander went to Edinburgh to help Thomson sort out his valuable collections and to help him distribute them to various specialists for further identification and classification. Agassiz wrote the text and made the drawings of the starfish and sea urchins for *Revision of the Echini* in the reports.

The success of this expedition inspired Agassiz to become a member of a similar American oceanographic expedition at the first opportunity. This came a year later in 1877 when the director of the U.S. Coast Survey asked him to take charge of a series of dredging cruises on the 350-ton schooner *Blake*. After looking over

Hatchetfish, torchbearers of the deep.

25

his new command, Agassiz made a number of changes such as substituting steel cable for the hemp rope used in deep-sea dredging and improving upon dredging and trawling gear. Agassiz's innovations saved much time and the steel cable took up less space on the decks. He was able to cut by two-thirds the *Challenger's* record-time of deep dredging.

Although he usually became violently seasick every time he set foot aboard a vessel, this malady did not deter Agassiz from the pursuit of his dreams. He was out of his bunk at 5 a.m. every morning to direct dredging operations in the search for unknown specimens from the deep sea. He supervised the setting of gossamer-thin nets to trap the crystal-like microscopic plankton and duly recorded the position and depth of each haul.

The *Blake* worked the waters around Cuba, Key West, Yucatan, and the Tortugas. Agassiz gave great attention to detail, as did Maury before him. Both knew that only from the steady accumulation of bits of detail could a whole picture of the sea be assembled. Agassiz was not averse to putting his knowledge of the sea to practical use. He thought the cold depths of the sea would make a natural refrigerator. Putting his idea into action one day, he lowered a bottle of champagne 2,500 fathoms only to discover on bringing it up to the surface an hour later that although it was cold the bottle was now filled with bitter salty water. The great pressure of the ocean had forced out the cork. "All that good champagne wasted on the fishes," Agassiz lamented later.

By the end of the first season, Agassiz had occupied 200 stations and made 230 hauls at depths ranging from 100 to 2,500 fathoms. His collections were so large that they almost rivaled those of the *Challenger*. With the enthusiasm of a boy trading marbles or cards with his friends, Agassiz wrote to Thomson to ask if he would like some of his specimens. "In one haul," Agassiz told Thomson, "124 rare sea lilies were brought up. I thought I would jump overboard when the tangles came up with them." Between cruises, Agassiz went back to the Harvard Museum to supervise classification of his specimens and the shipments to Edinburgh as well as running the mines from afar.

In the summer of 1880, Agassiz left on his third oceanographic cruise—to sound the depths of the Gulf Stream. He found animal life very scanty from Georges Bank to Charleston, S. C. His most exciting discovery was dredging up evidence that at one time the Caribbean Sea was an arm of the Pacific Ocean, which helped, in turn, to explain why the fauna of the West Indies was more like that of Central America than of the southern United States.

He also expected to find extinct geological or fossil forms in the deep seas but was disappointed when he found no evidence of these. He did correctly picture the bottom above the continental shelf (at a depth of 600 feet or less) as being carpeted with brilliantly colored marine animals. (Later underwater photography by Beebe in his bathysphere and by modern aqualungers proved him right.) "In contrast to the brilliantly colored animals of the shallow water," he wrote, "the deep sea floor is a monotony only relieved by dead carcasses of animals which find their way from the surface to the bottom and which supply the principal food for the scanty fauna found living there."

He made many trips during the 1880's to the warmer climates in hope of relieving his increasing circulatory troubles which had been aggravated while working in the mines years earlier. He was able to combine work and pleasure by planning a five-year expansion program for his Calumet mines which increased their output and made a fortune for him and other stockholders. He was now able to help needy students and give the Harvard Museum substantial sums of money.

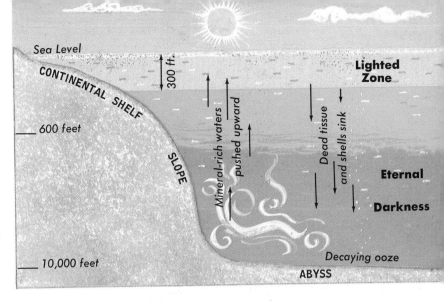

The lighted - or photic-zone near the surface is richest in plankton, fish and other forms of marine life. However, marine animals are found at all depths. The rain of dead, organic matter provides food for the intermediate and deep-sea dwellers. Upwelling currents bring mineral-rich waters to surface again to complete the cycle.

Labels in figure: Sea Level · CONTINENTAL SHELF · 300 ft. · Lighted Zone · 600 feet · SLOPE · Mineral-rich waters pushed upward · Dead tissue and shells sink · Eternal Darkness · 10,000 feet · Decaying ooze · ABYSS

Agassiz also found time to write a number of articles and books on his oceanographic researches. Each summer, he returned to his small marine laboratory at Newport, Rhode Island. When he received an invitation from the United States Fish Commission at the turn of the century to take charge of a deep-sea expedition along the Pacific side of Panama on the new 234-foot *Albatross,* he accepted.

Every morning as the dredge brought in a new haul, Agassiz would be on deck staring at each pile of deep-sea treasure, consisting of sharks' teeth, sea lilies and other bottom matter, as it was dumped on the deck. Some delicate forms were sketched on the spot and others were placed in vials for safekeeping. Not satisfied with working from dawn to dark, the men fished for plankton organisms at night, using electric lights to attract the tiny fish. As they swam toward the lights, they were captured in fine silk nets. Agassiz made two more trips aboard the *Albatross* into the Pacific covering Guam, the Fijis, Tonga, Cook and the Marquesas Islands.

During the last two decades of his life, Agassiz devoted much of his time to exploring tropical coral reefs which, like Gothic cathedrals, were ever building yet never finished. Agassiz disagreed violently with Darwin about the origin and growth of the coral isles. He called the author of *On the Origin of Species* "an armchair scientist," while postulating his own thesis that underneath every coral atoll or reef was an old volcano. But as time went on, it has been Darwin's coral reef formation theory of slow subsidence as the dominant mechanism that gained most support. In 1952 drillings at Eniwetok Atoll confirmed Darwin's predictions.

At age 69, Agassiz secured the *Albatross* for a third and last scientific sea voyage consisting of a 13,000-mile journey around Cape Horn and up the coast of Peru to Easter Island where he viewed the great stone images. His final ambition in life was to summarize all his cruises, sketch in the missing pieces of the jigsaw puzzle and then draw some conclusions about evolution. He employed up to 90 men at a time to work on his material, so tremendous was his desire to pursue all lines of investigation.

In the fall of 1909, Alexander and his son went to London where the elder Agassiz presided at a zoological conference. On his return voyage in March 1910, after an evening of cards and a conversation with friends, he retired to his stateroom where he died peacefully in his sleep.

His will left a large sum of money to the Harvard Museum and funds for the completion and publication of his unfinished lifework—the attempt to explain the biological and physical conditions of the oceans.

John P. Holland

The submarine, which has brought about the flowering of underwater oceanography, has reached its present high status through the sweat and vision of a series of American inventors going back to the Revolutionary War. The first of these was David Bushnell, a Connecticut Yankee, who built the first submersible designed for war. His tiny seven and a half-foot-long oaken craft, called the *Turtle*, unsuccessfully attacked the British man-of-war *Eagle* anchored off Manhattan Island in New York harbor on the night of September 6, 1776. The plan had been to attach a gunpowder charge to the hull of the British ship but the copper bottom of the warship prevented fastening the charge. General George Washington later referred briefly to Bushnell's invention, commenting that it exhibited a "touch of genius."

A quarter century after the *Turtle's* ill-fated adventure, another American inventor, Robert Fulton, known primarily for his contribution of the first practical steamboat, the *Clermont*, also brought his mind to bear on the problem of submarine navigation. While residing in France during the year 1800, Fulton secured a grant of 10,000 francs to build a 21-foot-long submarine named appropriately the *Nautilus*. After successfully demonstrating his invention in the Seine and at Brest, he pleaded with his French backers to allow him to use it to attack the British Fleet, but failed to obtain their consent. Even the British turned him down when he tried to peddle his device to them. Frustrated by the conservative naval thinking abroad, Fulton returned to the United States where he started to work on a giant submersible capable of carrying 100 men when death overtook him in 1815.

Although interest in submarines was revived from time to time, especially during the American Civil War, no notable advances were made due to the lack of adequate means of propulsion. Then late in the 19th century two new figures took over the center stage in the developing submarine-design picture. One of the men who played a dominant role in the struggle for the acceptance of the submarine as a recognized vessel for warfare was named John Holland. The other was Simon Lake who began constructing submarines in 1894 with peacetime uses primarily in mind.

John Philip Holland was born at Liscannor, County Clare, in 1841 and grew up with an Irishman's deep resentment toward England. As a young man he drew up plans for a submarine that he hoped could crush England's sea power. In 1873 school teacher Holland emigrated to America because he was hampered by a lack of money to complete his dreams on the eastern shores of the North Atlantic. At first his prospects of moving ahead with his submarine ideas in the New World appeared dim but took a turn for the better when at age 35 he received some welcome funds from the notorious SINN FEIN ("Ourselves Alone"), an Irish secret society that was pledged to strike at England.

Holland completed construction of his first submarine in the Paterson, New Jersey workshop of his two compatriots, Messrs. Todd and Rafferty, in 1878. This first vessel *Holland No. 1* was launched on the Passaic River and performed a few test dives using borrowed power when her crude petroleum engine failed to operate. Holland was dissatisfied with the results and sank his brainchild on purpose when it became apparent that a larger, improved model was needed. Holland, nevertheless, had been able to use this first vessel to try out several of his innovations, such as using horizontal diving planes which could control the depth of his boat under the surface, and subdividing water ballast tanks to insure safety and stability of the vessel when the hull was at an angle.

Holland's second vessel was built at the Delamater Iron Works at the foot of West 13th Street in New York City, and launched in May 1881. Named the *Fenian Ram*, the three-man submarine dived almost daily in New York harbor, performed much better than her inventor had expected and attracted wide interest. Financial troubles and factional strife within the Fenian Brotherhood ended the tests of the *Ram* and any chance of using it against England.

In the ten lean years that followed, Holland was unable to gain the backing needed to advance his ideas into a practical vessel. Married and with little real income since having abandoned teaching, he continued to work on his paper dreams. At one low point he turned his talents toward designing a steam-powered flying machine. No backers were forthcoming and he returned to his submarine designs.

Holland, who usually wore a black derby hat on a head that was distinguished by a large walrus-like mustache and pince-nez eyeglasses, conceived his submarine as a vessel which would submerge beneath the surface on its engine power in a condition of neutral buoyancy. Other inventors working on submarines thought of an underseas craft which would descend on an even keel with a slight negative buoyancy. His competitor Simon Lake saw the submarine as a potential oceanographic exploratory vehicle which could roam the bottom of the sea if the water were not too deep. Thus it was not strange that his first experimental vessel was equipped with wheels and an air lock for sending out a diver.

In an open competition for a Navy contract to build an operational submarine Holland won out over Lake and Thorsten Nordenfelt, a machine-gun inventor, who had built a steam-powered submarine in Stockholm in 1883. The Navy ordered that the completed submarine possess three propellers with a steam engine to propel it on the surface and electric motors to power it beneath the waves. Holland had doubts

The Fenian Ram, *Holland's first successful submarine, now stands in a park in Paterson, New Jersey. The clean porpoise-like lines of this early underseas boat closely resemble hull designs of the latest U.S. nuclear submarines.*

that the government's specifications would produce a satisfactory underseas boat. After many delays and reversed decisions the Navy finally, in 1893, awarded the newly formed John P. Holland Torpedo Boat Company a $200,000 contract to build a submarine meeting the Navy's specifications.

As this first vessel, the *Plunger*, began to take shape in Baltimore, Holland's reservations were vindicated. The time required for extinguishing the fire and venting the steam in the boilers made the period of preparation for diving too long to insure the safety of the crew in combat. Furthermore, the heat remaining in the firebox even after the hot coals were extinguished made the interior of the boat unbearably hot when the vessel was submerged. Before the *Plunger* was ready for launching Holland told the government officials that their steam monstrosity would be useless.

Fortunately his Company had already embarked on a gamble at its own expense and had constructed an improved submarine designed by Holland without Navy interference. He proposed that this submarine be substituted for the *Plunger* and that the Navy send official observers to witness the next trials of the new Holland boat. In his new submarine the inventor scrapped the steam-powered approach for a gasoline-engine-driven vessel which could be shut down instantly by the throwing of a switch and the transfer quickly made to battery-powered electric motors for underseas operation. The porpoise-shaped craft had been built at the Crescent Shipyard, Elizabethport, New Jersey in the winter of 1896-97. After two years of sea trials and testing the U.S. Torpedo Boat *Holland* was finally accepted by the U.S. Navy on April 11, 1900. The gamble on an unapproved design had paid off and marked the beginning of an enduring and profitable relationship between the Navy and the Holland Company.

This was the sixth submersible built by the persistent Holland and the first ever to be accepted as a regular element of any navy. At the time neither Holland nor the Navy realized that just half a century later more sophisticated versions of his original creation would assume the roles once held by the mighty battleships of World War I and the aircraft carriers of World War II.

Holland's revolutionary vessel was 54-feet-long, just over 10-feet in diameter and

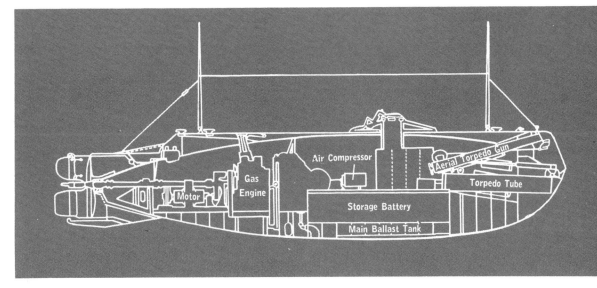

Plan of 53-foot Holland, *the U.S. Navy's first submarine.*

displaced only 75 tons when submerged. The 45-horsepower gasoline motor was connected to a dynamotor which charged the batteries on the surface and served as an electric motor when submerged. In place of the later-developed periscopes, Holland used windows in his conning tower for sightings above the surface which meant that the captain could only scan the surface of the sea by bringing the submarine to a "decks awash" condition. The ship also was equipped with a White torpedo tube and an aerial torpedo gun in the bow which led to the *Holland*'s recognition in naval circles as a legitimate submarine-warship.

The favorable notices and successful test operations of the *USS Holland* ultimately brought a renewed order for six more underseas craft to the Electric Boat Company which was the name of the new syndicate which had taken over the patents to Holland's inventions and absorbed the Holland Torpedo Boat Company. Unfortunately, this management change led to an unhappy turn of events. Repeated quarrels soon ensued between Holland and the businessmen running the syndicate and the dispirited inventor of submarines was pushed aside as the firm depended less and

less on his talents. Production of fleets of submarines had become more important than design changes.

Britain soon recognized the importance of Holland's breakthrough and since she had no submarine designers of her own, she purchased plans from the Electric Boat Company to build her own underwater vessels. There was a touch of mystery surrounding these plans, however. It turned out that the plans submitted by the Electric Boat Company were unusual in details and in some cases obviously in error. The first of five Holland subs ordered into production almost turned turtle at its launching and four of the completed boats met with major accidents which took 30 lives. Some thought that John Holland's early Irish loyalties might have some connection with these events but this is considered unlikely. Whatever the cause of these failures the conservative Admiralty was not convinced that this new type of vessel was yet ready to challenge the battleship as Mistress of the Seas, so the Royal Navy did not move to integrate submarines as a vital working part of the fleet.

Japan, locked in a mortal struggle with Russia in 1904, took a different view. She contracted directly with Holland, who was now selling his designs independently, for five high-speed submarines and with the Electric Boat Company for five A-class submarines.

Her enemy, Russia, went to Simon Lake and purchased his submarine *Protector* and the A-boat *Fulton* from Electric Boat Company. Although the United States was neutral in that Far Eastern conflict, the American submarine firms were ingenious in selling their vessels to the combatants in a disassembled state. Lake even traveled all the way to Russia where he assembled his submarine and trained its initial crews. The original Lake underseas boat, the first of five purchased by the Russians, was shipped by the Trans-Siberian Railway to Vladivostok to serve as an element of the defense of that key Pacific harbor. Neither the Lake nor the Holland boats saw any action in the Russo-Japanese War. Hostilities had ceased before they could be tried in combat.

Final testing had to await the coming of World War I. In the second month of the war a German U-boat would sink three British cruisers within one hour. All too swiftly the world would know the grim news of the *Lusitania* and the effectiveness of undersea warfare. Ironically, a year before the Irish-American inventor's death

in, August 1914, his most noteworthy achievement, the *USS Holland*, was sold for scrap. His first successful nuts-and-bolts creation was being dismantled just as a new dimension to ocean warfare was being added.

Holland spent his last few years withdrawn from public life. Legal action taken by his former company prevented him from competing in U.S. and foreign markets. For a time he occupied himself with sketches for a pleasure passenger submarine which would give the public a chance to view the undersea world. In his writings he discussed such peacetime uses of the submarine and its potential as a craft for scientific research. It would take another 50 years, however, before man started in earnest on plans to adapt the submarine to peaceful exploration of the ocean's depth.

In his remaining years, Holland's caustic comments on developments by other submarine designers may have made him seem a tired and bitter man. No one, however, could deny his early vision and contributions to the development of undersea craft. In the pantheon of great submarine inventors, beginning with David Bushnell and Robert Fulton, through Simon Lake, John P. Holland stands at the top of the conning tower.

William Beebe

For 15 years in the mid-20th century, a slightly built American ornithologist and explorer held the world's deep-sea diving record. Charles William Beebe, who rarely used his first name, captured the admiration of adventurous people around the world when he descended with his friend, Otis Barton, over a half-mile down into the Atlantic in mid-1934 in a spherical-shaped diving chamber which was known as a bathysphere.

Upon their return to the surface of the Gulf Stream, Beebe further sparked the imagination of future oceanauts with his vivid descriptions of the changing colors of the depths of the sea as he and his partner descended deeper into the abyss. "The sun is defeated, and color is banished forever, until a human at last penetrates and flashes a yellow electric ray into what has been jet black for two billion years," he said.

Beebe, a native of Brooklyn, New York, attended Columbia University. He joined the New York Zoological Society in 1899 where he became curator of ornithology—in charge of bird life. After 20 years of collecting and caring for birds, he was promoted to the post of Director of the Department of Tropical Research, where he remained until his retirement in 1952.

As part of his work, he made many expeditions to Central and South America, the Orient and the West Indies. Of the ten books which he published during his career, the majority were concerned with birds and jungle life, but his most famous was *Half Mile Down* which vividly retold the story of the descent into the abyss with his partner, Otis Barton.

William Beebe had broadened his field of expertise to include marine life some years earlier. Several oceanographic cruises

33

and countless descents in heavy diving gear to observe the teeming life of the coral reefs off Bermuda had made Beebe aware of the limitations of existing techniques for the study of marine life. Looking for solutions to the problem of exposing a man to the extreme pressures found at depths below 300 feet, Beebe borrowed from the exploits of Alexander the Great. The ancient king was said to have observed the ocean floor while submerged in a glass barrel covered with asses' skins. Beebe involved engineer-designer Otis Barton in the idea of a deep sea observation chamber and Barton designed and financed the construction of a sphere which they hoped would enable them to explore the deep-sea. Unlike Alexander, whose safety was assured by the angels, Beebe and Barton would depend on steel, quartz, oxygen and rubber to protect them.

The steel ball designed by Barton was only four feet nine inches in diameter and weighed 5,400 pounds. It had three round windows made of three-inch-thick fused quartz, the strongest transparent material known. Oxygen was provided by two oxygen tanks, along with trays of calcium chloride to absorb moisture, and soda of lime to remove excess carbon dioxide from the air. This cramped bathysphere would be supported and serviced by a derrick and winch-loaded ship on the surface, via a 3,500-foot-long steel cable and telephone line, which obviously limited its mobility below the surface. Aided by funds from the New York Zoological Society and private grants, Beebe procured a large, open-decked barge, called the *Ready,* to serve as a mother-ship.

By the summer of 1930, after a year of building and design changes, the bathysphere was ready for testing. The strange craft was placed aboard the *Ready* and towed to the lee side of Nonsuch Island off Bermuda, where for years Beebe had been studying the life of the deep sea. The two adventurous inventors were excited at the prospects as they scanned the skies on June 11th to check the weather for their first manned deep descent, after several successful dry runs made without passengers and a manned test which had taken them to 800 feet.

After being bolted inside their cramped quarters, they were lowered over the side of the *Ready.* Beebe described the eerie descent as the last visible link with the upper world slipped away; he felt a sense of complete isolation, as though he were in a plane lost in outermost space. As they descended below their previous record level of 800 feet the light gradually faded. Beebe noted the changes in ocean coloration: "In turn the red, orange, green, and blue rays disappeared, leaving only the faintest tinge of violet. Then there was only a blackish-blueness until at 1,000 feet every trace of light was gone. Below this depth the world was blacker than black."

As they sank into the sea's night the first flashes of animal life appeared. At first indistinct and distant, they became larger and more abundant as the diving sphere went deeper. The creatures which caused the moving patterns of irridescent lights could not be seen. Then Beebe turned on his electric searchlight to reveal a bright array of silver hatchetfish. Beyond 1,000 feet the luminescent light of the marine animals themselves, flickering outside of their quartz windows as dots or balls of fire, added to the bathysphere's artificial light. Upstairs, a secretary, Gloria Hollister, seated on the deck of the *Ready,* took down copious notes as she listened to Beebe's verbal description relayed to her over the telephone.

In poetic terms, Beebe described the feeling that came over him as they descended even deeper into the abyss: "... There came a moment which stands out clearly, unpunctuated by any word of ours, with no fish or other creature visible outside. I sat crouched with mouth and nose wrapped in a handkerchief, and my forehead pressed close to the cold glass—that transparent bit of old earth which so sturdily held back nine tons of water from my face. There came to me at that instant a tremendous wave of emotion, a real appreciation of what was momentarily almost superhuman, cosmic, of the whole situation; our barge slowly rolling high overhead in the blazing sunlight, like the merest chip in the midst of the ocean, the long cobweb of cable leading down through the spectrum to our lonely sphere where, sealed tight, two conscious human beings sat and peered into the abyssal darkness as we dangled in mid-water, isolated as a lost planet in outermost space. Here, under pressure which, if loosened, in a fraction of a second would make amorphous tissue of our bodies, breathing our own home-made atmosphere, sending a few comfortable words chasing up and down a string of hose—here I was privileged to peer out and actually see the creatures which had evolved in the blackness of the blue midnight which, since the ocean was born, had known no following day; here I was privileged to sit and try to crystallize what I observed through inadequate eyes and interpret with a mind wholly unequal to the task. To the ever recurring question: 'How did it feel?' . . . in the words of Herbert Spencer I felt like 'an infinitesimal atom floating in illimitable space.' No wonder my sole written contribution to science and literature at the time was: 'Am writing at a depth of a quarter of a mile. A luminous fish is outside the window.' "

After an hour of submergence in which they went down 1,426 feet, over a quarter of a mile, Barton signaled to the *Ready* to raise the bathysphere. Soon thereafter the two underwater pioneers stepped out on the decks of their mother-ship with the "memory of living scenes in a world as strange as Mars." A wave of emotion gripped Beebe as he realized that man had been able to survive these tremendous underwater pressures at immense depths.

Two years later, Beebe decided to go even deeper—twice as far as he and Barton had gone before. But, during August 1932, his first attempts were plagued by winds, storms, and leaks in the bathysphere. Finally on September 22nd, the balding Beebe and his partner Barton wiggled through the tight hatch and descended below the level of all measurable light. "From here down, for two billion years there had been no day, no night, no summer, no winter, no passing of time

William Beebe's steel bathysphere.

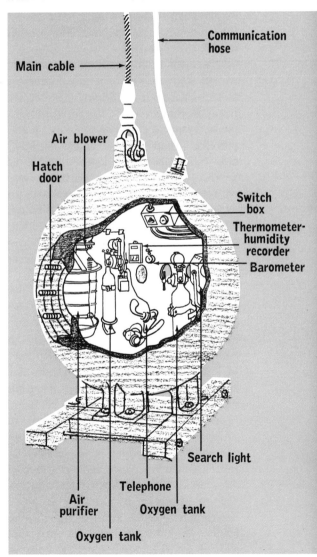

until we came to record it," he reported by telephone to Miss Hollister on the deck of the *Ready*.

He was surprised to find life more varied and abundant in the deep sea than he expected. Over a period of six years he had made several hundred net hauls in the same area, but he misjudged the actual quantity of sea life at the various levels until he went down to see for himself.

At a quarter mile down the sea was thick with living things. From there to 2,200 feet, the deepest point reached on this second series, there was hardly a moment when there wasn't some kind of life crossing the man-made cone of light outside their window.

The dives in the bathysphere were not without mishap. On their initial deep-dive a leak developed around the entrance hatch. Beebe phoned to the surface to drop the bathysphere quickly hoping that greater pressure would seal the hatch. Luckily it did. Twice the sphere came up from unmanned tests with the compartment flooded; once when a quartz window broke and again when the door did not seal.

After the 1932 dives, Beebe exhibited his bathysphere at the 1933 Chicago Century of Progress Exposition where more than half a million people viewed it. Following the exhibit, the National Geographic Society offered to sponsor a new deep-dive. In August 1934, after a thorough overhauling and repainting of the bathysphere from white to blue to serve as camouflage, Beebe and Barton once again climbed into their tiny home and prepared to descend to new, record depths. From the jellyfish that he saw near the surface to the squid, pale round-mouthed eels, great red shrimp, giant angler fish, saber-toothed viper fish, and silver hatchetfish seen at the lower depths, Beebe kept up a constant stream of narrative telephonic description of the strange sights down below. At 3,000 feet, the sea was aglow with living fire, as fascinating unknown

species of fish, their bodies aglow with what seemed a multitude of tiny flashing lights, swam by.

He saw giant 20-foot-long fish without eyes or fins, fish with green, glowing sides and long chin tentacles, fish with five distinct lines of yellow light surrounded by purple lamps running the length of the body. The spectacle was comparable to any fireworks display on earth. Beebe was completely intoxicated as he used up all the adjectives in his vocabulary to describe these weird creatures.

After two hours below, in which he reached the record depth of 3,028 feet, he asked to be hauled up. As he returned to the world of men, he felt like a sleepwalker in a state halfway between fancy and reality. When, after several hours, he was able to throw off his dream, he reviewed his notes and dictated characteristics of the undersea creatures to the shipboard artist who made drawings of what Beebe had seen below.

Beebe felt that the three outstanding dramatic moments in his dives were the first flash of animal light, the eternal darkness, and the discovery of new species of animals. He summed up his adventure with the statement: "The only place comparable to these marvelous nether regions must surely be naked space itself, far out beyond the atmosphere between the stars." How right he was in his prediction, made a quarter of a century before the Space Age was born!

This was his last series of deep dives. Thereafter he made a number of short dives. He conducted more than 60 expeditions of all types from deep into jungles to the ocean depths until his death at age 84 in June 1962 at Trinidad, where he had been working at the New York Tropical Research Station. He will be remembered best as the man whose exploits in the bathysphere focused public attention on the vastnesses of the sea and the richness of the fauna within it.

Hyman G. Rickover

In March 1953, after the launching of the nuclear powered submarine, *USS Nautilus,* the ship's "father" received a Legion of Merit commendation from Navy Secretary Dan Kimball. It stated: "He has accomplished the most important piece of development in the history of the Navy." The Secretary was referring to the efforts of a little known, white-haired, Navy captain who overnight had changed naval warfare. His name was Hyman Rickover.

The coming of the atomic bomb and the successful postwar tests in 1946 on U.S. naval surface ships at Bikini caused the navy to look beneath the waves for its future military missions. As the battleship was the queen of the seas in World War I, and the aircraft carrier in World War II, so the submarine had been thrust upon center stage as the new capital ship of naval warfare.

The Navy at first seemed unwilling to acknowledge the presence of the atom and

had been unenthusiastic about atomic weapons since the days of the Manhattan Project, which created the first atomic bomb. President Truman's Secretary of the Navy fought energetically against the use of atomic bombs against Japan. The Navy even protested the artificiality of the Bikini experiment in 1946, arguing that under combat conditions, ships would not be grouped that close together. They felt that the A-bomb would probably have no strategic or tactical uses in naval warfare, but would be restricted to land use.

For Admiral Mahan in the late 19th century and the generations that followed him, sea power was essentially a thing to be used at sea against enemies on the sea and those near the sea. The post-Mahan Navy was shaken by the advent of nuclear technology, but unfortunately most of the Admirals were unable to unshackle themselves from the traditions of the past. Since we were still the greatest military power in the world in all three elements—land, sea and air—with an atomic monopoly besides, complacency reigned among the heads of our services, until the Soviets exploded their own A-bomb in 1948. Our atomic monopoly had ended and the world would never be the same again.

In 1946 there was a slight indication that the Navy might bow to the changes of the atomic age. At Washington University in St. Louis, Chancellor Arthur H. Compton, one of the key scientists who developed the first atomic bomb, entered into a small contract with the U.S. Navy for a $103,000 study into the feasibility of harnessing atomic power for ship propulsion. The decision to begin this project was made in July 1946 midway between the atomic tests Able and Baker at Bikini. Compton put 40 scientists to work on the contract. The press misreported the story as a project to come up with a workable atomic unit to propel a battleship.

Actually the Navy had one person at least who foresaw atomic reactors as possible engines for submarines as early as 1939. The chief physicist of the Naval Research Laboratory, Dr. Ross Gunn, requested and received $2,000 for preliminary studies along these lines. The idea was shelved during the war and when NRL scientists tried to revive it at the war's end they were turned down by the Manhattan Engineer District, the organization responsible for all atomic matters.

The District was exclusively oriented to the atom as an explosive and any other application of the atom as a power reactor was a luxury project for the distant future. Furthermore, Lt. General Leslie R. Groves of the Army who commanded the District maintained a stifling cloak of secrecy around his project and would not give Navy officials clearance to obtain atomic information concerning controlled fission. If the Navy wanted data, he suggested they would have to join the Manhattan District. On March 14, 1946, this sug-gestion was affirmed by Secretary of Defense James Forrestal who agreed that the Navy should send a few qualified men to Oak Ridge to learn about reactors.

Thus, in April 1946, a short, graying Navy captain with a spare frame and tired-looking, hawkish face, reported to the atomic laboratory at Oak Ridge, Tennessee to study nuclear physics. He had been the only Navy captain who applied for the single Bureau of Ships billet to learn about the atom and its possible use in ship's propulsion. No other good sailor was interested, but Hyman George Rickover wasn't considered a good sailor. He preferred book reading to shore leave and disliked cocktail parties. His only sea-going command had been an old rust-bucket minesweeper which he piloted around the China Sea in the mid-thirties.

Many thought that Rickover did not even like the Navy, because of his un-willingness to abide by most of its concepts, methods, traditions, and institutions. Actually his love of the Navy moved him to change many of the outmoded ideas. He saw that a crusade to build a new and more powerful Navy had to start first with the destruction of the old one.

Rickover was born on January 27, 1900, in Russia. While he was still a boy, his parents emigrated to America and settled in Chicago where his father ran a tailoring business. Upon graduation from a local high school, he accepted an appointment as midshipman at the U.S. Naval Academy.

After graduation from Annapolis in 1922, he served five years aboard the *USS Lavalette* and the *USS Nevada,* but then returned to Annapolis to pursue a postgraduate course in electrical engineering. After obtaining a master of science degree in electrical engineering from Columbia University in 1929, he was assigned to the Navy's sub-base at New London, Connecticut where he served on the submarines *S-9* and *S-48.*

In the fall of 1937 he assumed command of the *USS Finch*, a grimy minesweeper, and then reported to Cavite Navy Yard in the Philippines as Engineering Officer. In 1939 he returned to the United States and spent most of World War II in the Bureau of Ships in Washington as head of the Electrical Engineering Section. (He received the Legion of Merit for his outstanding, unsung work in this post.)

Rickover arrived at Oak Ridge with his command of four young officers and the glimmering of an idea that the ideal ship for a nuclear-propulsion unit was a submarine. Rickover knew the limits of the submarine. Having served as a submarine officer he realized that subs were tethered too tightly to the short-lived electric storage battery and the marginal air-breathing diesel engine. The average submerged speed of our submarines in World War II was a pitifully slow three knots, which was kept down so as not to drain precious batteries. The necessity of surfacing at night to recharge batteries made conventional submarines vulnerable to enemy attack. The heat released from fission of Uranium 235 could drive a steam propulsion system that would not require outside air. The energy available in just one pound of uranium fuel was equivalent to 300,000 gallons of diesel oil. Rickover felt that submarines had most to gain from nuclear propulsion if it could be perfected.

He was quick to see that the existing large stationary reactors would be impractical aboard ship. He felt the Navy should design its own nuclear propulsion unit and so he wrote a letter to the Chief of Naval Operations in the summer of 1946 stating that he could build an operational propulsion plant in five to eight years. He added that if he were given adequate funding and enough technical talent, he could do the job in as little as three years.

His letter had no apparent effect for his proposal was ignored. A year later he wrote another letter to his superiors condemning the newly formed Atomic Energy Commission, the successor of the Manhattan District, which he charged was only interested in the production of fissionable material for bombs. He also blasted American electric-power industries for not having the foresight to invest in the research to develop an atomic power plant. This letter did set a few wheels in motion.

Rickover was called back to Washington, given a small office in a converted ladies' washroom and assigned to the Chief of the Bureau of Ships as a Special Assistant. But Navy interest in a shipboard reactor dwindled rapidly and the only study project undertaken consisted of a liquid-metal, heat-transfer system under the code name, "Genie" developed by General Electric.

Rickover was not to be deterred. He went to high ground for help—to the office of Admiral of the Fleet, Chester Nimitz, the Chief of Naval Operations, who was an old submariner. Rickover convinced the World War II naval hero that a successful reactor could be built and Nimitz agreed to support him. Nimitz wrote a letter stating that "the atomic submarine is militarily desirable."

Soon a Nuclear Power Division in the Bureau of Ships was established with Rickover in charge. But the battle was not yet won. Captain Rickover encountered stiff opposition from topside and below in the Navy echelons, but he had a newly won arsenal of weapons to protect himself from the petty brass who sniped at him. These peculiar weapons consisted of political, technical, scientific, and doctrinal support. Added to these were his own personal weapons including an enormous ego, tyrannical methods of operation, and an unrelenting pursuit of perfection.

Many colleagues disliked him because he was changing the Navy, was arrogant, Jewish and brilliant. Meanwhile, the AEC in late 1948 made a deal with the Navy and created a Naval Reactor Development

Division. Rickover was put in charge, which made him the boss of both the Navy and the AEC ends of the project. This move—giving him two hats—made it possible for Rickover to write letters to himself, answer them right away and get "agreement" for the official record. He even got the AEC to admit that a controlled nuclear reactor was "practical."

On July 28, 1948, he negotiated a contract with Westinghouse which had begun developing a more promising water-cooled reactor, using high pressure water as a heat-transfer medium, under the project code name, "Wizard." A year later the Chief of Naval Operations issued a formal operational requirement for the development of a nuclear-powered submarine. In August 1950, construction was begun on a shore-based prototype of the proposed *Nautilus* nuclear power plant.

Rickover recruited top men from industry and the university world as well as the Navy, offering them little but long hours and hard work. His grinding principle of operation was to enlist loyalty and encourage responsibility and individualism, with his eye always on the future. In return, his team worked for him with a fanatical devotion, knowing that their one great enemy was time. While work progressed on the nuclear sub, Rickover established an atomic submarine training school at the Massachusetts Institute of Technology and lined up top officers from the Navy's underseas fleet to enroll in the three-year training program.

Rickover built up a reputation for cutting through red tape. He once said, "A straight line is the shortest distance between two points, even if it bisects six admirals." But he got things done, despite being known as a "tyrant" and "despot."

While Rickover was presiding over a naval revolution in his office in Temporary Bldg. 3 on Washington's Constitution Avenue, a time bomb was ticking under him. In July 1951, the temperamental cap-

tain was passed over for promotion to Admiral by the Navy Selection Board. The promotion turndown reflected their judgment on Rickover's protocol manners (or lack of them), his race, his sandpaper temperament, and his challenge to naval tradition.

On June 14, 1952, Rickover, dressed in civilian clothes to avoid attention, stood in the rear of the crowd assembled in the Electric Boat Co. shipyard in Groton, Connecticut, while President Truman laid the keel plate of the first nuclear submarine. The day before the keel-laying, a second selection board had met in Washington and casting aside pleas of the Navy Secretary, the Chairman of the AEC, and, Rickover's own superiors in the Bureau of Ships, the board had again denied the hardworking captain his promotion. The board gave as its reasons for passing over Rickover's name a second time, the fact that he was "too specialized for promotion to the rank of Rear Admiral," and "precedent required a background in all-around duty." Then an outraged Congressman, Sidney Yates of Illinois, blasted the selection board for its motives and methods, charging it with "convoy mentality" and saying that it was geared to the slowest, most reactionary member of the group.

A Navy technicality was invoked to keep Rickover in uniform despite his turndown, but this did not satisfy the press or Con-

Cross section of the Nautilus.

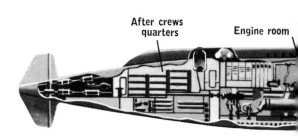

After crews quarters   Engine room

gress. By 1953 the Navy handling of the Rickover case had become a national scandal. Congress began to put pressure on the Eisenhower Administration in behalf of Rickover. The selection board that met in July 1953 was specifically directed to promote "one engineering officer experienced and qualified in the field of atomic propulsion machinery for ships." Only one man fitted that order, Hyman George Rickover, the first below-decks' officer ever to be named Rear Admiral in the history of the U.S. Navy!

Just before Mrs. Eisenhower christened the *USS Nautilus* in January 1954, a spurious rumor went around Washington, reputedly "leaked" by a high naval officer, that the atomic sub was merely a "test vehicle" with "little or no offensive capabilities." President Eisenhower fumed when he read the *Washington Post's* news headline: "Atomic Submarine Held Unfit for Battle NOW!" Secretary of Defense Wilson called in the suspected gold-braid culprits in the Pentagon to get at the bottom of the leak and read the riot act to them in a blistering six-hour session.

On January 17, 1955, the $40 million *Nautilus* cast off her lines and proceeded down the Thames River to the sea after signaling the historic message: "Underway on nuclear power." Rickover's compulsive persistence and time-chopping techniques had paid off. After the *Nautilus* went to

sea, Rickover's larger task began—to convince the Navy that the entire underseas and surface fleet should be converted to nuclear power.

Not only Pentagon brass were the objects of Rickover's attacks. This intellectual maverick also launched a crusade to update American education. He blasted educators for turning out youths who were handicapped by their lack of knowledge. To insure that properly trained technicians were available for his Naval Reactor Program, he established two special schools along European models.

Admiral Rickover was also involved in the selection of key personnel to man the nuclear-powered ships of the new Navy. To avoid friction with the powerful Bureau of Navy Personnel he outwardly downgraded his own part. Actually he played a key role through his famous stress and strain interviews in selecting future leaders of the U.S. Navy and not just handlers of "hot" nuclear equipment.

The end result of Rickover's drive and foresight was a fleet of underseas boats, armed with guided missiles that have been and still are a strong deterrent to any attack against the United States. He also made it possible for others to begin plans for undersea exploration, deep-sea submergence, and other oceanographic research projects that were unthinkable before the nuclear submarine.

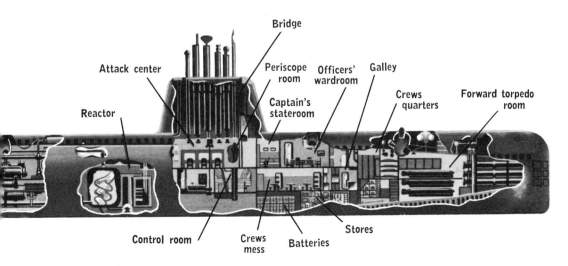

Bridge

Attack center

Periscope room

Officers' wardroom

Galley

Reactor

Captain's stateroom

Crews quarters

Forward torpedo room

Control room

Crews mess

Batteries

Stores

SHIP'S POSITION

U. S. S. *NAUTILUS*

TO: COMMANDING OFFICER

1915 U | 3 August 1958

90° 00.0' N | Indefinite

☒ NGA ☒ | MK19

Honolulu 4844

North Pole | Zero

180 | MK19 | 3E MK23 | 170 E

☒ | 244 359

William R. Anderson

In 1964 a young Democratic Congressman was elected to the House of Representatives from Tennessee, one of two men sent to our national legislature that year who possessed an engineering degree. For William R. Anderson, USN (Retired) this step into politics was far different from the feat that put his name into the history books. For Representative Anderson, while serving as a Navy Commander in 1958, piloted the first submarine ever to make a transpolar voyage under the Arctic ice cap.

That year was a momentous one for Commander William R. Anderson, the crew of the nuclear submarine, *USS Nautilus*, and the U.S. Navy. Their sub was named after Jules Verne's fictional submarine in his *Twenty Thousand Leagues Under the Sea* and Sir Hubert Wilkins' conventional underseas vessel of the thirties. The gallant Wilkins failed to take his sub-

marine to the North Pole in 1931 because of insurmountable obstacles. After World War II a young physicist named Dr. Waldo Lyon, who worked at the Navy Electronics Laboratory in San Diego, perfected an inverted fathometer device which allowed echoes to bounce upward from a submarine to the ice blanket overhead in a frozen sea. His successful experiments with this revolutionary device made it possible for other men to start thinking about the possibilities of a nuclear-powered submarine traveling under the ice.

The first nuclear-powered underwater submersible was the American *Nautilus* which was completed in 1955. By 1957 this pioneering vessel under another commander had already covered 137,000 miles in test voyages and was now ready to show that she could perform a challenging and dramatic assignment. It was under

Anderson's command that the *Nautilus* met that challenge and the long dreamed of first transpolar voyage became a reality.

Anderson, the son of a farmer, was born on June 17, 1921, in Bakerville, Tennessee. Although this handsome youth with smiling eyes grew up far from the ocean, he yearned for navy life and was happy to receive a Congressional appointment to Annapolis in 1938. He received a bachelor of science degree in electrical engineering in 1942 and then went immediately to the Navy Submarine School at New London, Connecticut. Most of his subsequent naval career was spent in submarines, beginning as a communications officer on the submarine *Tarpon* where he participated in seven war patrols in Japanese waters in early 1943. During this phase of World War II he received his first award for helping to sink 21,000 tons of enemy shipping. Later on in the conflict, he served aboard the submarines *Narwhal* and *Trutta*. Upon the outbreak of the Korean War, he returned to the *Trutta* as executive officer and then was given command of his first sub, the *Wahoo,* in Korean waters. Anderson is best described by a fellow officer as a man "who always had his crew behind him despite being a 'spit and polish' commander."

In 1956 Anderson was ordered to Washington for a six months' tour with Captain Hyman Rickover at the Naval Reactors Branch after passing the future Admiral's tough two-hour-long interview in which he tested candidates with tricky questions about their resourcefulness and imagination. Anderson and Commander James Calvert, who was later to surface with the nuclear submarine, *Skate,* near the North Pole soon after Anderson had completed his epic first, were both subjected by Rickover and his staff to a crash training program on navigation in polar latitudes and under pack ice. Anderson and Calvert also learned about the operation of nuclear reactors and turbines.

After nearly a year of study and discipline in Rickover's Naval Reactors Branch (which was run jointly by the Atomic Energy Commission and the Navy), Anderson was ordered to take over command of the 320-foot-long *Nautilus* from Captain Eugene Wilkinson, her first captain. He soon found himself in possession of the most modern submarine afloat, Among other conveniences were a library of 600 books, a photo darkroom, a movie theatre, foam rubber mattresses in the bunks and a juke box. On June 19, 1957, the *Nautilus* headed up the east coast of North America toward the ice cap lying between Spitzbergen and Greenland with official orders reading: "At discretion, proceed under the ice in the vicinity of 83° North Latitude and return." Anderson knew that the decision as to how far one could go in interpreting the word "vicinity" was up to him. He might even go to the North Pole, if he felt it was humanly possible for his crew to accomplish this feat. As he neared Jan Mayen Island, a trackless, unbroken, white desert of ice appeared on the horizon and Anderson knew it was time to submerge.

As the *Nautilus* pushed northward under the ice pack, Anderson often scanned Dr. Lyon's inverted fathometer looking for a rare polynya, or overhead lake, in which his submarine might surface. He was amazed at the 50-foot-long fingers of ice that extended below the ice blanket like stalactites hanging from the roofs of underground caverns. While attempting to surface after spotting a streak of light in the ice, the *Nautilus* damaged both periscopes on solid ice, and the ship had to hurry back to the edge of the ice pack where the crew surfaced and repaired the damage to their twin eyes. All went well on the return trip under the ice until their comfortable watertight cocoon reached 83° N. Then a fuse in the ship's gyrocompass blew. After trying to navigate on magnetic compasses, Anderson reluctantly had to turn back after finding himself playing "longitudinal roulette" spinning around in an endless circle under the ice. Although Anderson had failed to reach his goal, the North Pole, he had passed latitude 87° N., a record arctic penetration by ship.

In June 1958, almost a year later, after the *Nautilus* had run her first 62,000 miles equal to Verne's 20,000 leagues under the sea without refueling, Anderson was ordered to make a new attack on the arctic ice. This time the *Nautilus* would try a trans-polar passage from west to east by traveling through the Bering Sea and across the Arctic Ocean to Greenland.

En route to Seattle through the Panama Canal, a number of minor problems arose, such as a stubborn leak in the condenser, a small fire and mysterious fumes which resulted in a forced surfacing. The *Nautilus* had orders to remain unidentified until her mission was completed, so the first night at sea after leaving Puget Sound, Anderson

had the big white numbers 571 on her conning tower painted over. As the ship dropped below the surface of the Pacific Ocean after clearing the Strait of Juan de Fuca, Anderson picked up the mike and relayed a dramatic message to his crew over the ship's public address system: "All hands, this is the Captain speaking. Our destination this trip is Portland, England, via the North Pole!"

The spirits of the crew rose as they cruised quietly, with no sign of motion, at a pleasant 72° F. internal temperature. After threading her way through the Aleutian Islands, the *Nautilus* passed through the Bering Sea and began the task of finding passage through the ice-choked Bering Strait. On the first attempt the *Nautilus* found herself sandwiched so tightly beneath the ice that only 43 feet of water lay between the keel of the ship and the ocean floor, while less than 25 feet lay

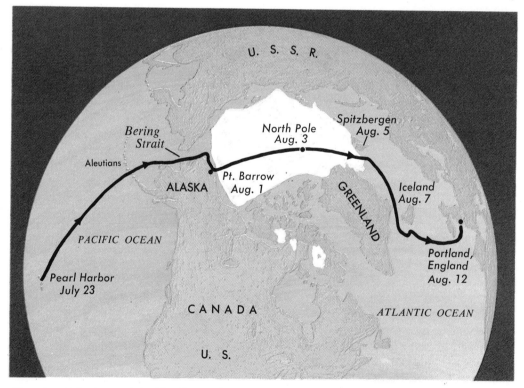

Map shows the route of the Nautilus *as she forced the first passage beneath the ice of the Arctic to reach the North Geographic Pole in August 1958. Two earlier attempts by Anderson failed.*

between the hanging curtain of ice overhead and the top of the ship's sail.

Finding the western approach closed, Anderson changed course and tried again, further east. This time he found easy clearance through the strait. Now they were entering the Chukchi Sea where the landmasses of Siberia and Alaska form a funnel to trap the floes of arctic ice. Proceeding slowly northward, the *Nautilus'* sonar revealed even deadlier ice ahead. Anderson, seeking somehow to force a passage, delicately dropped his ship to a depth of 140 feet, just 20 feet above the ocean floor. Slowly the ship cleared a huge block of ice overhead by a scant five-foot margin.

Tension remained high as the men stood at their stations, knowing that the ice might be thicker up ahead and the water shallower which might mean that they would be entombed forever if the *Nautilus* became jammed in an icy vise. It was soon apparent that the way to the Arctic Basin was blocked and Anderson decided to turn back once again. Disappointed, he radioed Admiral Arleigh Burke, the Chief of Naval Operations, for instructions, realizing that it was heartbreaking for him and his crew to accept the fact that the first attempts to reach the North Pole underwater had ended in failure. Burke ordered him to Pearl Harbor, Hawaii, with the crew sworn to secrecy about the object of the mission.

Not a word leaked out from the crew after their welcome in Hawaii. Back East for a quick visit with his family, Anderson received reports that the ice had receded considerably and he felt that it might now be safe to try to make another try for the Pole. On July 22nd the *Nautilus* found herself again underway after leaving her base at Pearl Harbor. This time she had new equipment on board such as closed-circuit television to observe the ice overhead. Soon the blue, tropical waters of the Pacific gradually gave way to the cold gray breakers of the frigid north. As the sub once again entered the treacherous waters

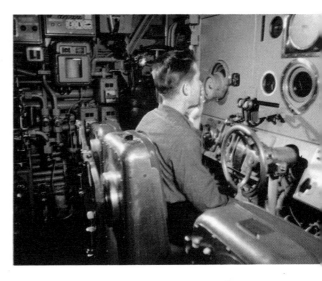

A crew member at the controls of the Nautilus.

of the Chukchi Sea, Anderson joyfully reported that, where before it had been jammed with ice, it was now free.

After dodging hazardous blocks of ice, the *Nautilus* reached 70 degrees and 45' North by July 30th. As it made its way under water toward Point Barrow, Alaska, long, icy stalactites which had broken from the pack above loomed in the path of the ship, causing her to change her course several times. But to the relief of everyone on board, the water was deep enough here for the ship to clear the lethal ice. On August 1st the *Nautilus* sailed under the true polar ice pack and a great weight was removed from Anderson's shoulders as they moved into deeper water of the Barrow Sea Valley and comparative safety. He now felt free to tell the crew that the *Nautilus* would attempt a crossing of the North Pole. The slogan among the crew soon became "North Pole or Bust!"

Dr. Waldo Lyon, the oceanographer who was also aboard, collected daily scientific data on the ice, particularly the pressure ridges hanging 100 feet below the level of the main body. His deep water fathometer was at the same time measuring the true depth of the previously uncharted Arctic Ocean floor, which ranged from 500 to 2,100 fathoms. Deep gorges were found ringed by steep cliffs, rugged mountain ranges and flat plains, similar to relief forms found on dry land.

The men who were off duty could watch the ice passing overhead, like moving clouds, on the television set in the control room. For the 116 men aboard, the high point of the epic voyage was near, as the Captain announced over the PA system: "All hands, this is the Captain speaking. In a few minutes, the *Nautilus* will realize a goal long a dream of mankind—the attainment by ship of the North Geographic Pole. With continued godspeed in less than two days we will record an even more significant first—the completion of a rapid transpolar northwest passage from the Pacific to the Atlantic Ocean."

Anderson glanced at his distance indicator. He began the dramatic countdown as they neared the Pole: "Stand by, 10, 9, 8, 7, 6, 5, 4, 3, 2, 1, Mark! August 3, 1958! Time 23:15 (11:15 EDST)." Then for the record he noted that the temperature of the water outside the submarine was a cold 32.4° F. and the depth to the floor some 13,410 feet. The crew coined a new word for this remarkable achievement "fan-damntastic" and that's just what it was.

A hilarious North Pole party was held in the ship's mess complete with an appropriate cake and a Santa Claus who berated the crew for invading the privacy of his home during his vacation season. Commander Anderson, with a sense of history, wrote a radio message to President Eisenhower at the height of the party on this "journey of importance" and one to the First Lady who had christened the *Nautilus*. The message to the Chief of Naval Operations said simply: *"Nautilus 90° N."* He planned to send the message as soon as they found a polynya large enough to surface. "Captain," cracked one of the crewmen with a grin, "we should have brought some carrier pigeons with us."

After reaching open water northeast of Greenland, on August 5th, the ship surfaced and proceeded to a secret rendezvous at Iceland. There Commander Anderson was picked up by helicopter and flown to Washington where President Eisenhower released the news to the world and congratulated him and his crew for their feat. He rejoined his ship a few days later at Portland, England, where they were given a tremendous welcome. A short time later, the gallant ship entered New York harbor on a misty, rainy day. Admiral Rickover met the ship as it received the whistles of the tugboats and fireboats. He rode into the harbor past the Statue of Liberty with the proud crew. For this moment in history, the *Nautilus* was the most famous ship in the world. By her transit across the roof of the world, the *Nautilus* had at last found the northwest passage which had eluded mariners for hundreds of years.

In the course of its historic voyage, the *Nautilus* made the first continuously recorded echo-sounder profile across the center of the Arctic Basin. Anderson and his crew discovered that the bottom topography of the Arctic Ocean is for the most part that of a normal oceanic basin, with flat abyssal plains, scattered ridges and sea mounts and several rugged mountains. The greatest depth discovered on the 1,000 mile transpolar journey was just about three miles.

Anderson later wrote a book about his journey under the Pole. It was appropriately titled: *Nautilus, 90° North*. In September 1959, he was promoted to Captain, the rank he presently holds as a retired naval officer. Before retirement, he had the satisfaction of knowing that he had played a significant role in plotting the future course of the U.S. Navy. For the thrust of the *USS Nautilus* under the arctic ice not only opened up a new era of naval warfare and underseas transport, but significantly aided future navigation and exploration by submarines of the forbidding Arctic.

Auguste and Jacques Piccard

In Brussels, Belgium, during the late 1930's, a tall, white-maned, bespectacled Swiss scientist began plans for a new kind of deep submersible which he called a "bathyscaphe." It was based on an idea that had been with him since his student days—to send a balloon-type vehicle down into the sea instead of upward into the air. Professor Auguste Piccard, the world-famous inventor had already achieved a claim to fame in the annals of man's early probing of the stratosphere. In the early thirties he soared to then record heights of over 55,000 feet above the earth in a spherical gondola suspended beneath a large gas-filled balloon. His scientific contributions concerning the characteristics of cosmic radiation and other phenomena were considerable.

World War II interrupted any chance of carrying Piccard's plans for a workable submersible through to completion. Once the guns of war were stilled, however, the elder Piccard resumed work on the project. Aided by funds from the Belgian Government he and his son, Jacques, completed the first bathyscaphe, *FNRS-2* in 1948. (The original *FNRS* was the balloon which had carried its designer 11 miles above the earth.) Two unmanned test dives off Dakar proved the worth of their craft. Their bathyscaphe functioned according to the ancient Archimedean principle. This principle stated that any body immersed in a gas or a liquid is buoyed up by a force equivalent to the weight of the body; if less than that of the ambient fluid, it will float; if heavier, it will descend.

In his search for an economical substance lighter than water, Auguste Piccard rejected metallic lithium and ammonia as

47

too expensive and exotic. He finally hit upon a practical lightweight substance of low compressibility that was universally available—high octane aviation gasoline. Thousands of gallons of this cheap fuel were needed to fill the blimp-like float before it could function properly.

The queer looking bathyscaphe was really nothing more than a combination of a cylindrical float and a sphere able to withstand the tremendous pressures at depths several miles below the surface of the ocean. The watertight sphere, weighing ten tons and capable of holding two men, was suspended beneath the clumsy gasoline-filled cylindrical float which gave it the necessary buoyancy. Just as a balloon requires ballast to help pull it down, the bathyscaphe carried tons of iron pellets in order to submerge. To return from the depths, the ballast was dropped and the gasoline float would lift the sphere to the surface.

Piccard's early bathyscaphe, the *FNRS-2,* was bought by the French Navy for conversion into a prototype deep-sea vessel. Following this sale, the Piccards built a larger bathyscaphe which they called the *Trieste.* It underwent a successful manned dive off Italy in September 1953, reaching depths below 10,000 feet.

One wonders why it took twenty-five years from the perfection of Beebe's bathysphere to the development of a deep-sea submersible like the *Trieste.* The problem lay with perfecting safe ways of overcoming the difficulties caused by the increase in the pressure of the water as one descends into the ocean depths. Without adequate protection man would be crushed to a pulp and his submersible would disintegrate like an empty matchbox being shattered with a hammer. The pressure of the ocean is measured in tons and not pounds per square inch at the deep levels below 1,000 feet.

In 1954 Jacques and his father submitted a proposal to the National Science Foundation in Washington offering collaboration with American oceanographers and suggesting a series of deep dives in the Puerto Rico Trench. Although their proposal was turned down the Piccards did not lose hope of eventually finding a sponsor for their latest invention.

They knew that their brainchild possessed many advantages over all previous methods of deep-sea research, the most important of which was the provision for a means of direct visual inspection of the ocean floor and the creatures of the abyss.

In 1956, the *Trieste* was lying in drydock in Italy while the younger Piccard searched for funds for a new series of dives. He had earlier tried to interest the U.S. Navy but had received very little encouragement. Although the *Trieste* rested only twenty miles down the coast from Naples, the headquarters of the U.S. Navy's Sixth Fleet, only one American naval officer took the trouble to come to see it during its first three years of existence.

Dr. Robert S. Dietz, a civilian oceanographer stationed with the Office of Naval Research in London, first saw the possibility of America's putting the vessel to practical use. Dietz had met Jacques Piccard in London at a conference on underwater technology and was impressed with the quiet confidence in the intense dark-eyed young man. Dietz convinced him that the U.S. Navy might be interested in the scientific potential of the bathyscaphe. Dietz accepted an invitation to visit the *Trieste* at Castellammare di Stabia and some months later met Piccard on the Sorrento Peninsula where they walked together through the war-scarred Naval-meccanica shipyard to view the *Trieste.*

Piccard pointed out to Dietz that this radically designed submersible, as intricate as a fine Swiss watch, even had its own built-in "fail safe" device. In case of a power failure, the electro-magnets holding the iron pellets, which served as ballast while the bathyscaphe was beneath the surface, would release the ballast auto-

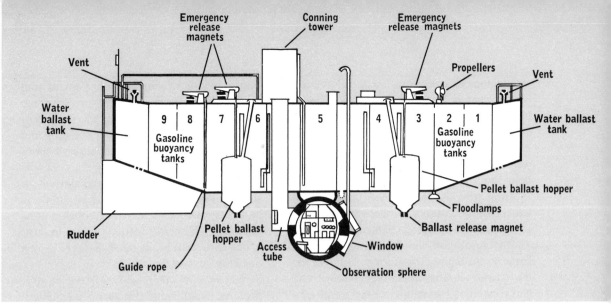

Cross section of the Trieste *showing her compartmented gasoline float and observation gondola.*

matically and send the ship immediately back to the surface.

The combined efforts of the aged physicist father, who had provided the initial design concept and calculations, and the son, who was an oceanographic engineer, impressed the American visitor. Dietz was particularly entranced with the successful 10,000-foot dive made by the *Trieste* in 1953. Realizing that the only other competitive bathyscaphe in the world was owned by the French Navy further prompted Dietz's interest. Jacques told him that he did not have enough money in his thin budget to buy a sonar echo sounder, a most critical instrument used for effecting a soft touch down on the seabed.

As Dietz reminisced later, "Everyone knows that submarines should be built by governmental alphabet agencies, technical task groups, contractors and subcontractors. Technical breakthroughs are not supposed to happen outside of well-financed laboratories. Modern technology is supposedly too sophisticated for backyard Edisons."

The irony of the situation was conveyed to the American who knew that his country, one of the two most powerful nations of the world, was then spending millions in public funds to place an unmanned satellite in space, while two land-locked Swiss citizens, with only private assistance, had succeeded in building a practical vehicle to take man to observe the deepest holes in the ocean.

Jacques Piccard was a 20th century version of Jules Verne's 19th century fictional submarine skipper, Captain Nemo, who operated a bizarre underwater vessel, *The Nautilus,* to take man where he had never been before. Dietz became charged with Jacques Piccard's contagious enthusiasm and soon they were journeying together to the United States where they could plead their case before several other civilian scientists in the geophysics branch of the Office of Naval Research.

The Office agreed that the operational potential of the *Trieste* as an underwater weapon was nil, but that her oceanographic capabilities were boundless. The U.S. Navy needed more knowledge about oceanography and this vessel might be the answer to its problem. They also realized that the U.S. submarine service would probably be able to obtain valuable technical spin-off benefits from the *Trieste's* high-pressure engineering devices. These would have many applications on deeper-diving submarines to be built in the future.

When the National Academy of Sciences sponsored a symposium in Washington, a year before *Sputnik,* on "Aspects of Deep Sea Research," Piccard and Dietz were included in the program to present papers on the bathyscaphe. The more than 100 top American oceanographers present were so impressed with their presentation that they adopted a resolution warmly praising the bathyscaphe's performance and favoring a national deep-sea program using such an undersea vehicle.

This resolution did not disappear into limbo as so many do, although support for the *Trieste* in the upper echelons of the Navy was not too strong. Some naval laboratory chiefs had misgivings about the bathyscaphe's possibilities and fell back on the traditional cheaper, easier and safer methods of gathering oceanographic data by unmanned wires and winches.

In February 1957 Piccard finally entered into a modest contract with the Navy aimed at further development and evaluation of the *Trieste.* A series of at least 15 summer dives was to be conducted in the Tyrrhenian Sea off Naples as the first American deep-sea experiments with the bathyscaphe. The 26 dives made by the *Trieste* in the Mediterranean between June and October were so successful that Piccard agreed to sell the bathyscaphe to the U.S. Office of Naval Research for the sum of $200,000.

Approval was finally given in late 1957 to purchase the bathyscaphe from Piccard, some two years after he and Dietz had first approached the Navy with the idea. In August 1958 the vessel was shipped to San Diego, California, and formally delivered to the Navy's Electronics Laboratory. Almost immediately, plans were made to modify the *Trieste* for dives deeper than before attempted. A new, stouter gondola was ordered from Germany and the float was enlarged to 34,000-gallon capacity. The remodeled *Trieste* was now ready for deep water dives.

On November 15, 1959 she attained a record depth of 18,150 feet in the

Pacific south of Guam with Piccard and Dr. Andreas B. Rechnitzer, an American marine biologist, making up the crew. But this warm-up only whetted the appetite of Jacques Piccard to take a seven-mile-deep plunge to the deepest part of the ocean. "Until man has placed himself on the bottom of the deepest depression on earth," argued Piccard, "he would not be satisfied. There is a driving force in man which will not be stopped if there is yet one step beyond."

When the great day arrived a few months later on January 23, 1960, America scored a triumph of exploration and oceanographic research when the *Trieste,* with Jacques Piccard aboard as pilot and U.S. Navy Lt. Donald Walsh as observer, descended 35,800 feet below sea level in the Mariana Trench of the western Pacific—the deepest ocean plunge that men had ever made.

All seemed well as they began their historic descent until the *Trieste* bounced upward several yards. She had reached the thermocline where the density of the deep water resists penetration of the ship. Piccard valved off some gasoline, and the *Trieste* once again began her descent into the blackness. Near the end of their epic journey several anxious moments occurred when a couple of mysterious cracking

Site of man's deepest dive, the Challenger Deep.

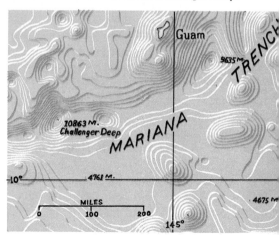

sounds accompanied by a rather heavy shock startled the two-man crew. They later discovered that the plexiglass window in the entry tube had cracked but fortunately it did not impose any danger to their compartment.

There was a possibility that they might collide with the trench walls before they slowed down enough for a safe landing. They were also concerned whether the bottom was firm enough for their bathyscaphe to land on or if they would disappear into a thick "soup" of mud and slime. After dropping some ballast they hovered for a moment three fathoms above a firm brown ooze. They could see the bottom in their searchlight.

They had reached the 6.8-mile-deep floor of the famous Challenger Deep off Guam after a five-hour descent in the cramped steel ball. The crew were completely unconscious of the 200,000 tons of pressure bearing on the *Trieste's* sphere. When they reached the bottom at 1:06 p.m. Walsh shouted to Piccard, "There it is, Jacques. We've made it!"

After they gently touched the ocean floor the two divers looked through their eight-inch plexiglass window. As they surveyed the carpet of ivory-colored silt which had lain almost undisturbed on the sea floor for centuries, the beam of their underwater spotlight showed a foot-long fish that looked like a flounder with eyes on the sides of its head. Later Piccard observed: "Here, in an instant, was the answer that biologists had sought for decades. Could life exist in the greatest depths of the ocean? It could!"

The two men shook hands and then contacted the surface ship using the special acoustic underwater telephone developed by the Navy. Another first had been accomplished—voice communication without wires between the surface and seven miles down. After 20 minutes on the ocean floor, making scientific observations, Piccard released 800 pounds of ballast and

the queer little underwater ship slowly began to ascend through the clouds of silt churned up by the ballast. Three and a half hours later the *Trieste* broke the surface, her mission over.

This historic dive which was part of the Navy's Project Nekton (named after sea life which can swim against the current) received only one or two columns of press notices in the world's leading newspapers. Few realized at that time that the *Trieste* had opened up a new and unknown territory for exploration, one which had previously appeared to be inaccessible. The seven-mile plunge to depths of the forgotten frontier signified a scientific advance that opened *all* the ocean waters to the exploitation of their resources.

Aged Auguste Piccard lived long enough to know that his son had descended to the deepest part of the ocean. He died a year later in 1962.

News of the *Trieste* was scarce for the next four years until word of a naval tragedy flashed around the world on April 10, 1963. The nuclear attack submarine *USS Thresher* had disappeared under 8,400 feet of Atlantic Ocean off Georges Bank, some 220 miles east of Cape Cod. Its crew of over 100 navy men and civilians were lost. Unable to find the remains of the shattered hulk by conventional means, the Navy had the *Trieste* transported overland from California to join the search. In August 1963 the little bathyscaphe, moving about on the ocean floor at 2 m.p.h., discovered the wreckage of the *Thresher*. The crew photographed the twisted debris and brought to the surface some remnants of the ill-fated vessel. The *Trieste* had proven her worth as an underwater detective.

Although the Soviets beat the United States in putting a man into space, we took the honor of being the first to launch men to the bottom of the sea, the culmination of the faith and drive of men like Walsh and the Piccards.

Rachel Carson

On April 14, 1964, a great American woman died quietly of cancer—just short of her 57th birthday. Her epitaph could best be described by a line of verse from the *Book of Revelations,* which underscored her philosophy of life: "Hurt not the earth, neither the sea, nor the trees." Rachel Carson, called by the *New York Times* "one of the most influential women of our times," won no outstanding prizes while she lived, nor did she personally lead any great crusade like Joan of Arc, Carrie Nation or Susan B. Anthony. Yet she personally attracted a tremendous amount of attention in high circles through the messages imparted from her concerned pen in a series of books which have left a continuous series of ripples as her real monument.

Rachel Carson was a shy, gentle spinster-biologist whose name has been conspicuously left out of the roster of the *American Men of Science*—because she represented the wrong sex. She proved a theory that shy people can be the toughest fighters for a cause worth fighting for. The human family all over the civilized world owes her memory a special debt of gratitude for her warnings of dire changes which man has made to disturb the delicately independent balance of earth's life forms on the land, sea and air.

Rachel Carson was born in Springdale, Pennsylvania, on May 27, 1907. She was brought up in this small town located a few miles northeast of Pittsburgh on the Allegheny River. The future biologist owed her love of nature to her mother, who taught her as a tiny child the joy in the out-of-doors and the love of birds, insects, and residents of streams and ponds.

By age ten, she showed her future literary talent as a contributor to the St. Nicholas League's publication. After she graduated from high school in nearby Parnassus, Pa., she enrolled at Pennsylvania State College for Women in Pittsburgh (now Chatham College) with intentions of pursuing a writing career. A course in biology revived her latent scientific inclinations, so she changed her major from English to science. After receiving a bachelor of arts degree in 1929, she entered Johns Hopkins University for postgraduate study. In 1930 she started teaching at Johns Hopkins and in 1931 became a full-fledged member of the zoology staff of the University of Maryland, where she remained for the next five years. (Meanwhile she received an M.A. from Johns Hopkins in 1932.)

Most academicians ultimately choose to specialize, and Miss Carson's career was no exception. She chose the oceans as her field of professional concentration. "Ever since childhood," she wrote, "I've been fascinated by the sea and my mind has stored up everything I have ever learned about it." She supplemented her studies in ocean life by undertaking special course work during summers at the Woods Hole Marine Biological Laboratory on Cape Cod. In 1936 she accepted a position in Washington, D.C. as aquatic biologist with the U.S. Bureau of Fisheries. The Bureau of Fisheries four years later became the U.S. Fish and Wildlife Service of the Department of Interior.

The Service's chief objective was to "insure the conservation of the nation's wild birds, mammals, fishes and other forms of wild life (both for recreation and economic value), with a view to preventing the destruction or depletion of these natural resources." Many of the bulletins and leaflets issued by the Fish and Wildlife Service were written by Miss Carson. She became Editor-in-Chief of *The United States Fish and Wildlife Service*, the official publication of the organization, in 1949. She held that position until 1952.

Her first literary writing on the sea and the life it sustains was an article entitled "Underseas" for the September 1937 issue of *The Atlantic Monthly*. Her brief but beautifully written essay on marine life was expanded and published in 1941 in book form under the title, *Under the Sea Wind*. This first book by Miss Carson gave a naturalist's picture of ocean life, with vivid descriptions of life on the seashore, the open sea and the ocean bottom in the Atlantic coastal area. The book was so popular that it was published in braille for blind readers and translated into several foreign languages. Miss Carson was a rare biologist who had found the knack of packing drama into each word and sentence of her writing.

During World War II the combined pressures of war work, coupled with new and revolutionary developments in the science of oceanography, caused her to postpone the completion of her second book, *The Sea Around Us*. "The conscious preparation for the writing of the book," she wrote, "involved the synthesis of a vast amount of research material." The actual writing of her classic work took over two years and covered several revisions. She wrote slowly, usually late at night after her work was completed at the Bureau office.

The first three chapters of *The Sea Around Us* appeared first in *The New Yorker* as a magazine essay entitled

"Profile of The Sea." When the book appeared in 1951 it was greeted by unanimous enthusiastic acclaim as the first attempt by anyone to capture the story of the seas and man's struggles to solve their mysteries.

In *The Sea Around Us* Rachel Carson revealed the science and poetry of the sea from its primitive beginnings to the latest scientific probings of its many tantalizing mysteries. She outlined different theories about the ocean's origins and behavior, describing the geography, history, chemistry and biology of the sea in layman's terms, enlivened with an exciting literary style of her own. The surface waters of the sea are described first, followed by a rundown of their variations and inhabitants and then progressing to the deeper waters and the sea bottom.

Miss Carson's work was adjudged to be a masterpiece with a style and imagination that made it a joy to read. It became a Book of The Month Club selection and went through dozens of editions, including paperback and deluxe illustrated, hard cover bindings. By October 1951 the unheralded work had become the number one non-fiction best seller and had progressed through nine printings. It later won the National Book Award as the best non-fiction work of 1951.

Her vivid poetic writing in *The Sea Around Us* illustrates why she won the award. Her description of her indirect encounter with the Gulf Stream while groping through the fog of Georges Bank for a solid week on the *Albatross III* in the summer of 1949 is a classic. "Those of us aboard," she wrote, "had a personal demonstration of the power of a great ocean current. There was never less than a hundred miles of cold Atlantic water between us and the Gulf Stream, but the winds blew persistently from the South and the warm breath of the stream rolled over the Bank. The combination of warm air and cold water spelled unending fog. Day after day the *Albatross* moved in a small circular room, whose walls were soft gray curtains and whose floor had a glassy smoothness. Sometimes a petrel flew, with swallow-like flutterings, across this room, entering and leaving it by passing through its walls as if by sorcery. Evenings, the sun, before it set, was a pale silver disc hung in the ship's rigging, the drifting streamers of fog picking up a diffused radiance and creating a scene that set us to searching our memories for quotations from Coleridge. The sense of a powerful presence felt, but not seen, its nearness made manifest but never revealed, was infinitely more dramatic than a direct encounter with the current."

In April 1951 she obtained a Guggenheim fellowship and took a year's leave of absence from the Bureau to start research on her third book, which would be a "study of the ecological relation of seashore animals on the coast of the United States."

Her plan was to produce a popular guide to help people to realize that "the beach is more than a place to get sunburned . . . Most people don't know where to look for the most fascinating things on the beach," she wrote. "All they can see are a few shells and an occasional crab. But there are all kinds of things going on right under the surface of the sand." This volume, *The Edge of the Sea* (1955), covered the natural history of the ocean shoreline.

Her greatest fame, however, came near the end of her life with her fourth and last book, *The Silent Spring*, which detailed the harm done to insects, animals, birds and fish by the indiscriminate use of chemical pesticides, such as DDT. The storm that arose by the publication of this book caused her to be likened to Harriet Beecher Stowe and the wave of indignation that followed the publication of *Uncle Tom's Cabin* of an earlier era. The resulting clamor of public concern shook up the Departments of Interior and Agriculture as well as the Pure Food and Drug Administration. Her critics accused her of distortion but the exposé led to a stricter governmental system to check and control the chemical contents of insecticides and pesticides so they would not cause needless injury to wildlife and human beings.

To her friends and colleagues, Miss Carson displayed a matter-of-fact attitude about life, but underneath she harbored a deep concern for the conservation of life. This slim, blue-eyed, brunette, who never married, possessed a good sense of humor. "In a minor way," she mused, "I am a disappointment to my friends who expect me to be completely nautical. I swim indifferently well, am only mildly enthusiastic about seafoods and do not keep tropical fish as pets." Among her favorite authors were Thoreau and Melville, both of whom inspired her.

Secretary of the Interior, Stewart Udall, felt that there were two compelling reasons why the message of Rachel Carson's books will be heard for many years. First, were her qualities of mind and spirit, which were particularly revealed in her books about the sea. Here she caught and held the attention of millions of readers because she combined a scientist's eye with the poet's sense. Udall called attention to the lyric quality of her prose in the passage from *Under the Sea Wind* where she wrote these memorable lines: "To stand at the edge of the sea, to sense the ebb and flow of the tides, to feel the breath of a mist over a great salt marsh, to watch the flight of shore birds that have swept up and down the surf lines of the continents for untold thousands of years, to see the running of the old eels and the young shad to the sea, is to have a knowledge of things that are as nearly eternal as any life can be."

Secondly, Udall admired the Thoreau-like stand that she had taken in writing *The Silent Spring*. Her basic convictions were restated simply and eloquently before a Congressional investigating committee in 1962. "I deeply believe," she said earnestly, "that we in this generation must come to terms with nature!" This philosophy also applied to the sea.

As our best known contemporary popularizer of the sea and oceanography, Rachel Carson performed a yeoman service by writing dramatic and much needed essays on the importance of the seas to mankind and his future. Her factual, informative and comprehensive survey books on the sea have already become her monument. Her vivid descriptions of the hidden mountains and canyons of the ocean deeps, the various sea-mapping expeditions and the ceaseless power of the winds, waves, tides and currents which came out of her pen in poetic phrases will be quoted 100 years from now.

Miss Carson was the first modern science-writer to illuminate the true meaning of the oceans to man, including the heritage of the sea that man carries in his body. She had that rare knack of being able to translate scientific jargon into clear layman's language on a subject that is becoming more significant daily in man's ever changing struggle for survival.

Even the prosaic seaweed reveals a richness of forms when studied closely.

Maurice Ewing

For nine months of the year Dr. Maurice Ewing, a Professor of Geology, directs Columbia University's Lamont Geological Observatory. The other three months he usually goes down to the sea aboard the University's 202-foot, three-masted schooner, the *Vema,* to learn more about how the earth was formed and what lies beneath the oceans. "The people of the Observatory think I get my vacation on the schooner," wryly observed the white-haired, craggy-faced Ewing, "and my colleagues on the *Vema* think I get my vacation at the Observatory." On one of his sea-going "vacations" in the Atlantic the prominent geophysicist was swept overboard by 50-foot waves in a gale. He was finally rescued after floundering for 40 minutes in the sea.

This leading interpreter of the earth's structure and of the Pleistocene Period, the million-year epoch before recent geological history, was the first person to take seismic measurements in the open sea. As a result of this probing by sound waves he was able to announce to the scientific world that only a 2,000-foot-thick carpet of ocean sediment and three- to four-miles of crustal rock lay between the ocean floor and the earth's mantle. This startling geophysical discovery has become the basis for several ambitious schemes to drill and sample the sediments from top to bottom and to drill through the basaltic crustal rock and tap the underlying mantle.

Dr. Ewing views the carpet of uncon-solidated sediments on the ocean floor as a geologic calendar in which is preserved the whole history of the earth. He has stated that: "As we punch deeper into the ocean sediment we may reach levels holding traces of the first animals...evidence of the earliest green plants and ultimately the primeval sediment of the earliest erosion marking the advent of water in the sea. The entire record is there in the most undisturbed form...and the dream of my life is to punch that hole 2,000 feet deep and bring the contents back to the lab to study them."

William Maurice Ewing was born in the small town of Lockney, Texas in 1906. A graduate of the Rice Institute of Technology in Houston, where he received three degrees, B.A., M.A., and Ph.D., Dr. Ewing first taught physics and geology at the University of Pittsburgh and Lehigh University before being appointed to Columbia University in 1944. Five years later he became Director of Research at Columbia's Lamont Geological Observatory to conduct geophysical investigations and oceanographic expeditions.

Ewing, who has received many honors since then, started the Lamont Observatory on a shoestring in 1949 with the aid of six students. Today the Hudson River oceanographic research installation, located at Palisades, N. Y., has 20 buildings, 300 scientists and students, and has expanded into one of the world's greatest centers for geological and marine research.

In July 1947 Ewing led the first of three successive oceanographic expeditions to explore the Mid-Atlantic Ridge on the Woods Hole research vessel, *Atlantis I,* a converted schooner. This research project was jointly conducted by the National Geographic Society, Columbia University and Woods Hole Oceanographic Institution. Ewing's purpose was to take his 146-foot, steel-hulled ketch on a journey to chart a large section of the famous 300- to 600-mile-wide submarine ridge that extended 10,000 miles from Iceland to the Antarctic.

The ridge separates the Atlantic Ocean into two big eastern and western basins roughly three miles deep. This massive ridge towers 7,000 feet above the ocean floor. It generally reaches up to within a mile of the surface and in a few places emerges as islands in the Azores, St. Pauls Rocks and Ascension Island. This fascinating geological phenomenon was discovered in 1873 by the *Challenger* expedition.

Ewing planned to make a continuous profile of the ridge with the aid of several devices, including a deep-sea trawl, corers, thermometers, TNT bombs, hydrophones and a deep-sea fathometer. The spartan facilities aboard the *Atlantis* made living and working more difficult than life on a submarine. Washing was done in salt water and eating and sleeping were almost impossible in bad weather.

On this trip Ewing was able to put into peaceful use a gadget that he had perfected a few years earlier for military purposes. Ewing had invented the famous SOFAR (Sound Fixing and Ranging) instrument in World War II while working at Woods Hole on a Navy contract. His device was based on the fact that a small bomb, fired at the right depth, may be heard by hydrophones across the entire width of the ocean.

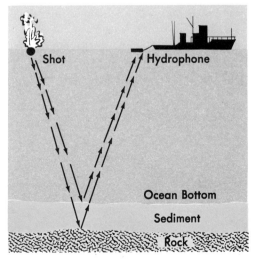

Ocean depth and thickness of sediment are measured by the return echoes from various layers.

With this device Professor Ewing developed an ingenious method of measuring the thickness of the layer of sediments that overlies the basement rock of ocean basins. He performed this feat by exploding depth charges and then recording their echoes, with one echo being received from the top of the sediment layer (the apparent bottom of the sea) and another from the "bottom below the bottom" or the true rock floor. Ewing used this method in exploring the Mid-Atlantic Ridge. He also used the seismic-refraction technique by which sound waves are made to travel horizontally through the rock layers of the ocean floor providing valuable information about their composition.

"Before these techniques were developed," wrote Rachel Carson in *The Sea Around Us,* "we could only guess at the thickness of the sediment blanket over the floor of the sea. We might have expected the amount to be vast if we thought back through the ages of gentle, unending fall, one sand grain at a time, one fragile shell after another, here a shark's tooth, there a meteorite fragment, but the whole conttinuing persistently, relentlessly, endlessly." In general, however, the sediments have proven to be much thinner than expected. This has led to speculation as to whether the ocean floor isn't somehow undergoing rejuvenation.

Interesting variations in the thickness of the sediment layer on the Atlantic Ridge and its western approaches were reported by Ewing. As the bottom contours became less even and began to slope up into the foothills of the ridge, he found that the sediments thickened, piling up into mammoth drifts 1,000 to 2,000 feet deep. Farther up the ridge where terraces several miles in width were found, the sediments were even deeper, measuring up to 3,000 feet. But along the backbone of the ridge on the steep slopes, peaks and pinnacles, the bare rock emerged swept clean of any sediments.

Ewing and his colleagues brought up piston corings with ocean sediments spanning 60 million years which marked the first time that sediments older than a few thousand years had been retrieved. During their survey they discovered a new underseas range about 50 miles long, 10 miles wide and 9,700 feet high, comparable to the San Bernardino Range in California. They also charted one underseas mountain peak higher than the Matterhorn.

Ewing was the first man to lower a deep-sea flashlight camera and take color photographs of marine life on the top of the ridge more than a mile beneath the waves. A year later (in the summer of 1948), he took the *Atlantis* on a second voyage to crisscross the ridge farther north and south. This time he made two back-to-back voyages covering a four-month period, sweeping over the Mid-Atlantic from Newfoundland to the bulge of South America.

After bringing up some prehistoric, white beach sand samples in his corer from a

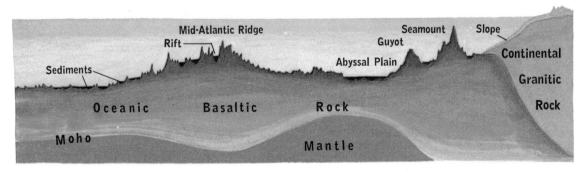

Generalized cross section of the Atlantic Ocean showing typical features of the ocean floor.

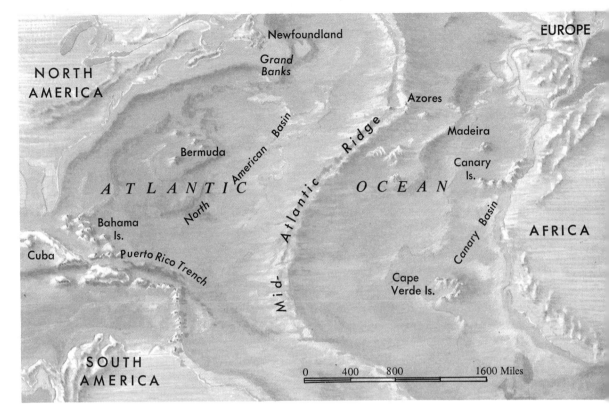

NORTH AMERICA

Newfoundland

Grand Banks

EUROPE

Azores

Madeira

Bermuda

North American Basin

Mid-Atlantic Ridge

Canary Is.

A T L A N T I C   O C E A N

AFRICA

Bahama Is.

Cuba

Puerto Rico Trench

Canary Basin

Cape Verde Is.

SOUTH AMERICA

0   400   800   1600 Miles

The dominant feature of the Atlantic Ocean floor is S-shaped curve of the Mid-Atlantic Ridge. The 10,000-mile-long range exceeds the Rockies in height.

three-mile depth Ewing speculated on the origins of the ridge and postulated that these finds, some running from 10,000 to 350,000 years old, proved that sections of the ocean floor must have been above water eons ago. This meant that the Atlantic Ocean could have been much lower than it is today.

On the second 1948 cruise the *Atlantis* lost two-and-a-half miles of expensive half-inch steel cable that broke suddenly after being weakened by excessive use and rust. Several members of the crew barely escaped serious injury by the backlash of the broken cable as it whipped across the deck. A week before Christmas the *Atlantis* lost the propeller of her auxiliary engine and her mainsail. Also lost were a dredge that became stuck under an underseas rock and the deep-sea camera which was accidentally heaved back into the sea. Despite

these mishaps the *Atlantis* managed to reach home three days before Christmas.

The present flagship of the Lamont Observatory is the *Robert Conrad*, a modern oceanographic research vessel built by the U.S. Navy and turned over to Ewing and the Observatory in 1962. She has made several extended cruises to sample sediments, and chart trenches and ridges which lie under the world's oceans. In pursuing her quest for knowledge the *Conrad* has sailed over areas in the Atlantic, the Caribbean and the Pacific not previously surveyed by oceanographic vessels. Dr. Ewing's special concern is collecting geophysical data which might give new insight into the nature of changes that have taken place in the earth beneath the sea during the past 4.6 million years.

When the ambitious Mohole Project of drilling through the earth's crust to the

59

mantle from a platform at sea became bogged down in engineering difficulties in 1963 Ewing saw that a great opportunity might be missed. He and two other prominent American oceanographers, Dr. John B. Hersey of Woods Hole and Dr. Roger Revelle, Director of the Scripps Oceanographic Institution, created a Consortium for Oceanographic Research and Exploration and asked the National Science Foundation for $10 million to build and operate a ship as an interim project "to explore the ocean sediments and upper crustal rocks and to test and develop techniques and devices useful for drilling the Mohole." But the Foundation did not go along with this proposal.

In August 1966 when further funds for the ill-fated Mohole Project were cut off by Congress, Ewing's idea appeared to be dead. But a year later a more modest deep-sea drilling project was unveiled when the NSF announced a $5.4 million grant to four institutions to drill a series of deep holes in the ocean floors in the most ambitious attempt so far to prove the much debated theory that the earth's continents were once joined together and have since drifted apart.

Called the Joint Oceanographic Institutions Deep Earth Sampling (or JOIDES) project, this new program combined the know-how of Ewing's Lamont Geological Observatory with that of the University of Miami's Institute of Marine Sciences, Woods Hole Oceanographic Institution, and California's Scripps Institution of Oceanography, which was named to direct the project.

Scheduled to get underway in late 1968, the JOIDES' backers proposed an 18-month, deep-sea drilling project at some 50 sites to bring up samples of rocks, fossils and sediment that could be examined for indications of the age and origins of the ocean basins. The plan is to conduct operations in the Atlantic and Pacific Oceans, the Gulf of Mexico and the Caribbean Sea

by sending drills through four miles of water and thence to penetrate up to 2,000 feet of sediment and earth crust. Among other findings the project directors hope to find an answer to the exciting issue which has caused controversy among geologists, i.e., the possibility that the ocean basins have been widening over the ages thus providing a contributing factor to the theory of continental drift.

During its 1966 summer voyage to plumb the depths of the North Atlantic, the Lamont oceanographic vessel, *Vema*, became the first civilian ship to fix its exact position on the ocean by means of orbiting satellites. Utilizing TRANSIT satellites whirling overhead in a 600-mile-high orbit to obtain precise navigational fixes and computers aboard ship, the *Vema* was able to reduce positional errors on oceanographic data from miles to just a few yards. Dr. Ewing, commenting on the success of the new devices, said, "I believe that the advent of the satellite navigation system marks the beginning of a new era in oceanography and in marine geophysics." The bushy-haired Ewing is now busier than ever supervising several expeditions at once and is perpetually "swamped" by the heaps of paper work required to run his complex operation on both land and the seven seas. He still has the same youthful urge and spirit that he exhibited over a quarter of a century ago when, as a neophyte oceanographer, he made his first exploratory ocean voyage out of Woods Hole.

As each deep-sediment corer and cable-held dredge is hauled aboard the various oceanographic ships of the Lamont Observatory new clues to the origins and makeup of the earth are brought to light. Major questions on the nature of the original crust, the possibilities of continental drift or convection currents in the mantle, and the very age of the earth, may well be answered in the next few years. This is indeed the time for geologists and geophysicists to be at sea.

Jacques-Yves Cousteau

"By the aqualung, photoflash and hand-held camera, we have been able to pull aside more fully the dense sea curtain which, since the dawn of time, has shrouded from man's eyes a world of vibrant color—the world of the twilight depths." Thus spoke the lean, bronzed man with the high cheekbones and a hawk nose who is considered by most authorities to be the primary moving force in the mid-20th century quest to find the answers to the mysteries of the ocean depths.

His name is Jaques-Yves Cousteau and this 58-year-old French underwater explorer and naval officer achieved immortality of sorts with his significant contribution to the field of oceanography by co-inventing the aqualung. This portable breathing device allows divers to swim like fish down to 300-foot depths in the ocean, unencumbered with cables, hoses and bulky diving suits. Cousteau, with the aid of a number of generous grants from the National Geographic Society, has made several color movies of his underseas adventures, which have helped to popularize the new art of skin diving and underwater exploration.

He has pioneered in the taking of color pictures under the surface of the sea and has salvaged the oldest known sunken ship in the world. This latter feat was accomplished in 1952 in the Mediterranean when a Greco-Roman cargo ship, dating from the 3rd century B.C., was discovered and its cargo of wine jars and Greek pottery was brought to the surface. His explorations are oriented toward utilizing the seas and their wonders for the benefit of mankind.

Jacques-Yves Cousteau was born in St-André-de-Cubzac, France. After spending one year in the United States as a boy, he returned to France where he ultimately entered the French Navy after graduating from the Naval Academy at Brest. His first interest in the world beneath the sea was awakened in 1936 at Le Morillon, when he saw underseas life clearly for the first time while wearing diving goggles. Thereafter, he spent many happy hours goggle-diving and fishing with spears. But this type of diving soon became unsatisfactory since he could not penetrate deeply into the ocean or stay under water for a long period. To overcome these deficiencies he designed a crude oxygen-breathing outfit to give himself more independent movement but soon had to discard his contraption when the use of oxygen alone caused convulsions.

During the German occupation of France in World War II, Cousteau carried on his diving experiments to conceal the secret work he was performing for the French underground movement. Late in 1942 he went to Paris to find an engineer to aid him in constructing a diving lung that would feed compressed air to a diver from three tanks strapped on his back. When Cousteau discovered that a fellow Frenchman, Emile Gagnan, had designed an automatic valve which embodied the desired principle, he got together with Gagnan and the two of them created the first working model of the aqualung. Their device was successfully tested in June 1943 off the French Riviera in the Mediterranean. Cousteau and Gagnan later improved their invention so that a diver could stay below more than an hour. Cousteau decided to test their new device at depths below 60 feet, trying it out during an investigation of a sunken British steamer, the *Dalton*. The aqualung proved to be safe and eventually the two men and their compatriots proceeded to extend the depth record to over 300 feet, a mark which held up for over 20 years.

At the end of hostilities in Europe after V-J Day, Cousteau became convinced that his diving experience might be useful to the French Navy. After showing films of his underwater experiments to the Marine Ministry, he was commissioned to train a team of divers in the use of aqualungs. He then assisted the French government in clearing away German mines that were blocking the harbors of southern France. His small group of expert aqualungers also made exploratory voyages into the Atlantic Ocean and Mediterranean Sea to study life below the surface as well as to conduct experiments, using themselves as underwater guinea pigs to test the effects of explosives on the submerged human body, among other things.

Cousteau's most dangerous moment under the surface of the sea during the post-war period came when he attempted to solve the mystery of the Fountain of Vaucluse near Avignon, a pool that erupts once a year for an unknown reason. The courageous Cousteau coolly descended into the fountain in August 1946 and almost perished at a 200-foot depth when he suddenly lost consciousness. Somehow, he managed to struggle to the surface and discovered to his dismay that his compressed air supply contained a mixture of deadly carbon monoxide.

In November 1951, Cousteau embarked on an expedition to the Red Sea in what was the first large-scale attempt to study undersea life, using the aqualung. Costeau acquired a war-surplus minesweeper which he renamed the *Calypso* after it was refitted with help from the French Navy as a laboratory and diving platform. The primary aim of this and subsequent expeditions to the Red Sea and Indian Ocean was to study and photograph marine flora and fauna in their true environment among the reefs and shoals of tropical waters. The research ship, *Calypso,* served as Cousteau's floating headquarters and marine science laboratory for many experiments, which ranged from tagging fish and studying their mannerisms to performing research on improving man's abilities to stay deeper under the surface of the sea for longer and longer periods.

A year after the first Red Sea expedition, Cousteau co-authored, with Frederic

Dumas, the classic book, *The Silent World.* In this inspirational volume the two aqualung divers described the "awe and beauty" of marine life under the surface and recounted their 16 years of experience as skindivers. Their book which was illustrated with some unusual color plates became a best seller and has been published in many languages. Cousteau has gone on to write a half dozen more books and has produced a dozen color films, including the poetic *World Without Sun* and *The Living Sea,* among others. He has won many honors over the years, including the Presidency of the World Underwater Federation, but he treasures most the dives he takes regularly with his wife, Simone, and his two sons.

In 1957 Cousteau was appointed the Director of the Institute of Oceanography and of the Museum in Monaco, which gave him a base for prophesying the future of man under the sea. Among other visions of tomorrow beneath the waves, Cousteau foresees: a highly developed underwater agriculture where animals will be bred in deep water ranges fenced in by nets; a world where chemistry will find a cheap method to remove salt from the ocean and make possible the purification of the rich soils accumulated in the salt water estuaries and render them available to man so that he may use them again. These and many more predictions of things to come have flowed from the mind and pen of this modern Mediterranean man who is not afraid of pushing man's destiny beneath the waves of the oceans.

The gaunt, graying Cousteau conducted a successful undersea living experiment in his *Conshelf One* (Continental Shelf Station Number One) in 1962 which marked man's first prolonged submersion in the sea. *Conshelf One,* consisting of a 17-by 8-foot dwelling unit and workshop, was anchored on the Mediterranean Sea floor, 40 feet deep, off the port of Marseille. It housed two men for a week. This breakthrough

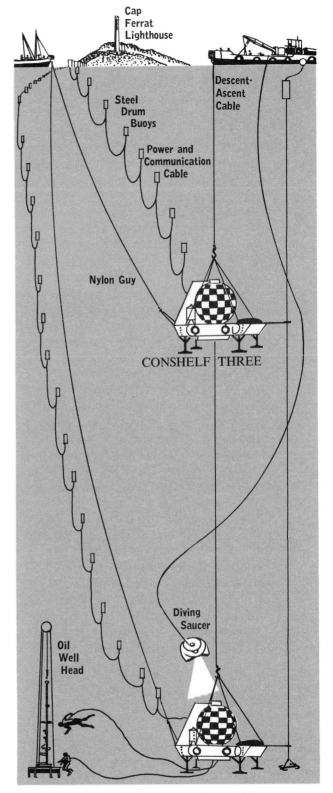

Conshelf Three *is lowered slowly 328 feet below the surface. A half-mile arc of steel-drum buoys supports power and communication cables.*

provided the spark that made possible the financing of the more ambitious *Conshelf Two* and *Three* experiments in the following years.

In his larger *Conshelf Two* experiment station Cousteau maintained five men for a month's submersion in the Red Sea during 1963 and proved the practicability of large-scale underwater living. Cousteau's two-man diving saucer provided an exploratory capability for the static underwater base. The pressurized station contained open bottom hatches into the sea below so his aqualung divers could swim out of their home and work in the sea for up to five hours a day. This second Conshelf station nicknamed "Starfish House" was located in the Red Sea, some 36 feet below the surface and a few miles up the coast from Port Sudan, one of the hottest cities on the face of the earth where the temperature often soars above 100 degrees. But, in their underwater home, the five aquanauts felt comfortable and cool at all times.

Above his undersea village, consisting of the four-armed Starfish House and its adjacent, onion-shaped garage containing the diving saucer, was Cousteau's chief supporting vessel, the *Rosaldo*. This vessel, floating on the torrid waters of the Red Sea, supplied air and power to the underwater abode via life-support hoses and cables that snaked downward to the *Conshelf Two*. Telephone and television links bridged the gap between the two worlds.

At the end of their 30-day stay in the Starfish House Cousteau's wife, Simone, swam down with a surprise birthday cake for her famous husband, and she and the crew celebrated the ending of another successful experiment. Cousteau summed up the importance of these experiments when · he said: "*Conshelf One* and *Conshelf Two* have convinced our underwater team that industrial and scientific seabed stations will become a routine procedure in our lifetime. A hundred practical applications undoubtedly will be found for submerged stations."

Some of these applications already awaiting large-scale exploitation include: oil drilling on the ocean floor; the mining of manganese, diamonds, gold, silver and other precious minerals; and the establishment of underwater research laboratories and production plants to process raw materials directly from the ocean and its bed.

Cousteau's most recent underwater expedition, *Conshelf Three*, witnessed six oceanauts staying for three weeks in a large undersea house located some 328 feet down in the Mediterranean off Cape Ferrat, southern France. They left their steel sphere daily to carry out their assigned undersea tasks while Cousteau remained on the surface keeping a constant vigil, by way of a television monitor, on his $700,000 project.

The spectacular color television documentary films which came out of this and subsequent expeditions helped to convince hesitant Americans who had expressed serious doubts about man's ability to live, work and sleep underwater. Cousteau has proved once and for all that, contrary to the pessimists who say that man is made to live only on land, with proper safeguards, he can exist and conduct himself underwater in a routine fashion. Cousteau has challenged us to help make the coming exploitation of the sea an orderly one and not the disorderly, unplanned, plundering kind that we have exercised on the surface of the earth during the past 500 years. The choice is ours.

To appreciate and understand fully the unique position which Cousteau currently holds at the summit of the new underwater elite, any oceanaut buff has only to read excerpts from one of his inspirational writings, *Homo Aquaticus*, to discern why he is held in such esteem.

"Primitive man feared greatly the watery medium of the earth, the oceans," he wrote. "The surface was always agitated, the water was generally cold, and the people died when they were obliged to stay in it for more than a couple of days. The pressure, of course, was a tremendous obstacle in itself. And fishermen, who were living on the sea, dreamed of monsters, or horrors emerging from the sea, of nightmares in this hostile medium. Nevertheless, efforts were made for a long time to do the impossible and penetrate the hostile, watery world."

Cousteau then classifies the points of departure which man has taken in his long-sought conquest of the sea. Beginning with the ancient naked divers, man has progressed through the more modern periods of diving bells, diving suits and aqualungs. But then Cousteau envisions the fifth and final departure, that of the future, which is the development of the new man—*homo aquaticus*—by surgical means. This stage, which is connected with space research, envisions men living under water who will be able to resist pressures down to 1,500 meters, and who will be able to move from the surface to this great depth mechanically or freely, and then return to the surface just as quickly with no decompression problem at all.

To do this, Cousteau believes man will have to fill his lungs with an incompressible liquid, a step already taken experimentally with lower animals. Then a whole new generation of man will be born, perhaps even in underwater hospitals where, upon birth, he will be operated on in much the manner of current space experiments. Great progress in this area has already been made in space research. It is considered possible, for example, to take blood from beneath the left arm and circulate it through a regenerating cartridge on a belt. Such developments portend a real space man, and later perhaps, an underwater man who will be free from the bonds imposed by respiration in the usual sense. This new species of man will not be confined to underwater, Cousteau feels. After

surgery, he will be able to walk perfectly well on land, still with the regenerating cartridge, changing it from time to time. The new man will be equally at home skiing on an Alpine slope or swimming in a submarine canyon. And never fear for volunteers. We have already seen that volunteers can be found for any purpose!

Cousteau paints a parallel of the sea mammals, like the seals, which have returned to the sea after having roamed the earth as distant cousins of dogs. And if we can ever solve the mysteries of the porpoise, whose ancestors were land mammals, then we may find clues to help man return to the sea also. Cousteau deeply believes in the future of man in the sea and constantly preaches to his ever-widening audiences to prepare themselves for the coming radical revolution that will take place when man goes down to the depths in greater numbers.

"I am convinced," he wrote, "that the main goal for the future of underwater exploration is not the discovery of new resources, but the discovery of new sources of inspiration. And, of course, we need better submarines, better lungs, better filling mixtures, but above all, we need scientists to understand, and poets, painters, architects, philosophers to express it. We need a thousand new words which have to be forged by imaginative people. We need to reform our way of thinking about the sea. We need to return to the sea."

So spoke the President of the World Underwater Federation in his address at the 1964 convention of the society. Today, Cousteau is recognized as the leading member of the triumvirate who are pioneering underseas living in earnest. The other two men are Americans, the tall and ruggedly handsome Captain George Bond, USN, and Edward Link, the inventor of the aviation trainer whose interests turned from the skies to the seas in the sixties.

Edwin A. Link

Some men just dream dreams while others act. Edwin Link is an example of a man who does both. Although he had spent most of his life looking skyward, his focus in more recent years has turned downward to the potentials under the sea.

When Edwin Link turned his inventive talents to the sea after retiring as president of the General Precision Equipment Corporation in 1959, he knew that three-quarters of our planet—the wet world of the oceans and seas—still awaited exploitation by man. Link, a stocky, gray-haired man, made his first national reputation as an aviation executive and inventor of the

famous Link Trainer. This ground-simulator device was adopted by the armed services for flight instruction. It has been used to teach more pilots to fly than any other means, and it made Link a millionaire.

Link was born in Huntington, Indiana, on July 26, 1904 and attended the Binghamton, N.Y. public schools. Although he never completed college, he attended the Lindsley Institute for a short spell and has been awarded several honorary university degrees. He founded the company which produces the Link Trainers in 1927, and served as president of the firm for almost two decades (1935-1953). He was later

Chairman of the Executive Committee of the Link Division of General Precision Instruments Corporation, an electronics combine which bought his firm.

Married, with two sons, Link became interested late in life in the wet frontier. When he retired from an active role in General Precision he was able to devote more time to his hobby of underwater archaeology. One of his first underwater projects was to explore the submerged remains of the ancient buccaneer city of Port Royal, Jamaica. Two-thirds of the pirate town and 2,000 of its inhabitants vanished within two minutes on the fateful morning of June 7, 1692 when it was shattered by an earthquake and slid beneath the sea. In 1959 Link sailed into the harbor of the present-day Port Royal aboard his specially designed research vessel, *Sea Diver*, to organize the first systematic attempt to unravel the wicked city's past. He and his divers retrieved hundreds of clues to life in 17th century Jamaica, bringing up relics of value to historians.

Not content with the current techniques and equipment for undersea exploration Link began to use his inventive talents in developing new approaches. He began working on portable decompression chambers for divers to use aboard ships. In 1962 Link launched an experiment with divers staying for long periods at deep, high-pressure depths. Using Link's revolutionary diving cylinder, Belgian-born Robert Stenuit lived 200 feet under the sea for 24 hours. Breathing a helium-oxygen mixture, Stenuit swam out of the hatch of the pressurized cylinder to explore his environment and then returned to his cocoon to eat and sleep. The long, deep dive off Monaco set a record at the time, and inspired Link to try for deeper depths.

Link bought 18 white mice from a pet store and successfully exposed them to pressures they would experience at a 2,000-foot depth in a tiny, specially constructed pressure chamber. Next, he decided to take three mice down to a simulated 3,000-foot pressure depth to determine how far man could safely go. Two mice lived through this test which proved to Link that man himself might eventually live and work at such depths. (Later, when Link loaned his miniature pressure chamber to Dr. Christian Lambertsen of the University of Pennsylvania, the medical school professor successfully brought 16 mice through a simulated 3,000-foot deep-sea pressure experiment and 21 out of 24 mice through a 4,000-foot depth.)

Link firmly believes that the loss of the nuclear submarine *Thresher* off the New England coast, in April 1963, drastically changed the course of our study of the oceans by emphasizing the increased need for an expansion of a young science—oceanology. This new word embraces both the older established fields of oceanography (the scientific understanding of the seas) and the challenging new field of ocean engineering (their use by man).

In the light of the *Thresher* disaster, the Secretary of the Navy appointed Rear Admiral E. C. Stephan, the head of the US Navy Oceanographic Office, as chairman of a high-level group to study the Navy's undersea capabilities. Link, who had just reached Monaco on his research ship, *Sea Diver*, was invited to participate in a 22-man group composed of the country's leading oceanographers, marine engineers and divers to come up with some recommendations as to future military policy under the sea. He left his ship in the Mediterranean port and flew to Washington.

Link knew that their deliberations would also have an important impact on non-military uses of the sea. "Indeed, a determined program of oceanology," he has said, "could change our world by focussing attention on the huge resources of the sea by pointing the way toward their use . . ."

He was thinking of the tons of valuable minerals, fuels and food which lie beneath the waves and await mankind's decision to convert his present role from a hunter in the seas to a farmer and miner of the seas. "Man remains in this realm on a par with the aborigines," states Link. He believes that some 490 billion pounds of fish could be harvested from the oceans each year, without harming the present "flocks," in order to help feed an over-populated world. This would be five times the present catch from an area of salt water where three-fifths of all life on earth exists. To achieve this goal, Link believes new methods of fish farming and scientific knowledge of fish reproduction will have to be attained.

Link foresees a major increase in obtaining valuable ores, gems and oil from the sea. Most important, he envisions the time when man will turn to the "last water-hole," the oceans, for his drinking water to quench his ever-expanding thirst. He even feels that someday soon we may be able to modify the weather, not by seeding hurricanes from airplanes to break them up but by preventing their formation in the first place. This could be done by building underwater baffles and dams beneath the ocean's surface to deflect cool water upward and thus lower the surface temperature which is one of the prime causes of tropical storms.

Link agreed to postpone his own ocean research in late April 1963 and signed on as a member of the Navy's newly created Deep Submergence Systems Review Group (DSSRG) to assist in formulating an underwater program that would be of importance to this nation in war and peace. Link and the other members of the group soon became aware of how badly the development of the seas had been neglected. Deep diving, salvage and rescue techniques had hardly changed at all during the past quarter of a century. It took the *Thresher* tragedy to focus attention on this and allied problems of underwater operations. Link and the DSSRG discovered that the *Thresher* did not carry a "sonar transponder" which would answer a search craft's own sonar (sound-pulse) in a similar fashion to a downed astronaut's capsule, nor did it possess a radio-equipped distress buoy that would rise to the surface and send an SOS. The long search for the *Thresher* accentuated this safety need on future submersibles.

But search was only one phase of the problem. Rescue was another. The Navy's depth limit for rescue at the time of the *Thresher* disaster was a mere 800 feet via an eight-man diving bell. This device was totally inadequate to bring up any of the *Thresher* crew even if they had been found alive on the ocean floor 8,400 feet down. Early in 1964 the DSSRG recommended as one answer to the rescue problem that a small aluminum submersible capable of descending to 6,000-foot depths be built within two years. Link and the others envisioned these small, battery-powered, underwater rescue vessels either being attached piggyback fashion to regular submarines or dropped to a disabled sub from an airplane or small ship. They also kept in mind the possible future civilian uses for such an underwater search-rescue boat.

Link suggested to the DSSRG that the Navy equip its subs with a kind of life raft mounted in streamlined pods on the top of the vessels' hulls which could be used in emergencies for crew escapes from sunken submarines. Link's proposed method of escape for beleaguered sub crews is an adaptation of his latest invention known as an underwater tent or sea igloo. "The system is built around a rubber, inflatable, balloon-like bag which will accommodate 22 people," Link explained. Stored in deck containers until needed, the bags would then be inflated with a high pressure helium and oxygen mixture. Crew members would then make a quick transfer with the final stage being a leisurely trip to the surface. On the surface the snug survivors would then radio for help to nearby rescue ships and aircraft.

Meanwhile, Link was still busy "moon-lighting" on the side with his own ideas of keeping men alive under the water for long periods outside of submarines. His man-in-sea concept provides inflatable, movable, underwater shelters for men working beneath the surface of the oceans. Using his specially outfitted research ship, *Sea Diver*, as a launching platform, he demonstrated his concept in July 1964, with Robert Stenuit and Jon Lindbergh as two human underwater guinea pigs. They remained submerged off the Bahamas at a 430-foot depth for just over two days and then spent three more days in a de-compression chamber on the surface before emerging into normal surface atmosphere. During the experiment, in which they proved man's capability of staying at great depths for several days, the two men breathed a combination of helium and oxygen. While Stenuit and Lindbergh were below, they performed several useful tasks —from taking pictures to taming several 100-pound groupers. The oversize fish be-came so tame that when one of the divers dropped his toothbrush, a grouper swal-lowed it.

The 32-year-old Jon Lindbergh (son of the famous American aviation pioneer) spends most of his time in San Diego, operating an imaginative underwater en-gineering company. He chose this new and exciting field after serving a hitch with Navy demolition teams and learning marine biology at the Scripps Institute of Ocean-ography.

Link's setup marked an advance and variation of the Cousteau/Bond approach to undersea living. While their submerged shelters, *Conshelf* and *Sealab*, were per-manent, his was mobile, which offered sev-eral advantages in underwater exploring. His underwater dwelling contained bunks, a telephone, food, instruments, an air supply, and space for diving suits. In June 1966, he conducted a follow-up experiment with

his underwater igloo at 600 feet. "And we will go even further," he commented. "Men living and working at greater depths in the future is of great importance . . . to obtain the food and resources from the ocean when they dry up on the land."

The official name for Link's dwelling is *Spid,* for "Submersible, Portable, In-flatable Dwelling." Its rubberized fabric walls are held up by internal air pressure which also keeps the water out at the bottom, since *Spid* is open at its base. Link described how his dwelling differs from sub-marines and bathyspheres. "Men who go down in sealed chambers can look but not touch," he said. "We are trying to put men down at great depths to dwell and accom-plish useful work. The age of exploration is not over yet. Exploring the ocean is like exploring space. There is usable, obtainable land on the bottom of the sea which is equal to the continent of Africa." His final ambition is to develop the means whereby men could go to any depths anywhere in the oceans and be able to perform useful work.

Link thinks that portable, economical undersea houses could be inflated to

Deep Diver, *developed by Edwin Link, allows divers to exit by way of a special "lock-out" chamber to do work in the ocean.*

balloon-like shapes with either a small door in the bottom or an open bottom like a tent. Pressure of the air or mixed gases inside would serve as a counterbalance to keep the sea out. One bothersome problem, Link admits, is how best to hold the gas-filled dwellings down on the sea bottom. He feels that this task could be accomplished either with weights or by fastening the houses to the sea floor. He foresees mobile homes, with their own power supplies, that could propel undersea workmen across the ocean floor as they repair and inspect undersea installation like oil pipelines and telephone cables. Link realizes that the present foam-rubber, wet suits worn by aqualungers in relatively shallow dives would not suffice for contemplated deep dives in the future. In conjunction with the U.S. Rubber Co., he has apparently found a satisfactory answer to keeping body heat inside the suit by the development of a new kind of material in which insulating air cells are sandwiched between thin layers of rubber.

Link's most recent activity in the pursuit of his goal has centered around his latest creation, the *Deep Diver* submarine, a miniature oceanographic research submarine which he and John H. Perry, Jr. built together. This small vessel, unlike other research submarines, possesses a special "lock-out" chamber which makes it possible for divers to exit and do work in the ocean. In dives off Grand Bahama Island the 22-foot-long *Deep Diver* is helping to pioneer new techniques as the first underwater taxi to transport divers to the bottom of the sea. The divers are able to move in and out of their pressurized compartment at will, with the aid of their scuba gear. The yellow-painted submarine, which looks like an overgrown sea lion, resulted from Link's persistent efforts and belief that the sea floor need not remain "off limits" to man any longer.

In order to do more in developing underwater technology aimed at the exploitation of the riches of the sea, Link believes that a civilian underseas agency parallel to the National Aeronautics and Space Administration is needed to coordinate and encourage activities in this field. The establishment of an underwater, "wet" NASA would appear to be imperative if America is to accomplish the dreams and desires of such oceanaut pioneers as Edwin Link. In this way, he believes, the security and wealth of our country can be strengthened in the critical years ahead.

With a look to the future, Link warns us about not becoming too enamored with our plunge into the cosmos at the expense of our plunge into the oceans. "Nor is our only horizon overhead in space," he says philosophically. "We have resolved to put human footprints on the moon, yet our efforts to understand the sea consist of a limited program which stresses only the scientific description of the oceans. We have not awakened to the exciting challenge of the wet world."

George F. Bond and M. Scott Carpenter

While Astronauts Gordon Cooper and Charles Conrad were riding *Gemini 5* to the conclusion of a successful eight-day mission on August 29, 1965, they chatted by radiotelephone with Astronaut Scott Carpenter. This in itself would not have been unusual except for the fact that Commander Carpenter was not at one of the ground stations of the global N.A.S.A.-Gemini network but was some 205 feet under the surface of the Pacific Ocean in a submerged Navy capsule called *Sealab II*. This strange-looking underwater experimental research station was moored 1,000 yards off La Jolla, California.

The historic communication between two capsules—one submerged and the other in space—did not mark just a casual connection between the nation's emerging space and underwater programs but the joining up of the two last geographical frontiers that man has yet to conquer. Both experiments, the Gemini and the Sealab, had similar aims: to test the ability of man to live and to perform useful work in a strange environment. Like space, the undersea region offers natural resources of great potential, and it is possible that the lessons learned on each frontier can benefit those working on the other.

The topside director of this man-in-the-sea experiment, and unofficial leader of a new breed of elite deep divers known as the "Descendancy," was a handsome naval Captain named George F. Bond. Like his colleague, Admiral Hyman Rickover, he had met with resistance in getting acceptance of his ideas. But Captain Bond, a medical doctor and an expert in problems of staying alive under the sea, was not easily deterred.

Bond is a strapping, adventurous, middle-aged Southerner with an M.A. in philology in addition to his medical degree. Before entering the Navy, he ran a hospital for mountain folk in Bat Cave, North Carolina, and did some chapel preaching on the side. Bond eventually ended up in the Navy Submarine Medical Research Center at New London, Connecticut, where he became its director. One of his first underwater medical experiments found him practicing free escapes from torpedo tubes in submarines bottomed more than 300 feet down—without wearing any diving lung or oxygen tanks.

Bond's personality has been described as being composed of unequal parts of Li'l Abner and Dr. Walter Reed. In the Navy he is known affectionately as "Papa Topside." At the bottom of the New London Naval Medical Center's 100-foot-deep submarine training tank, novice divers with oxygen tanks strapped to their backs would be surprised to find their Commanding Officer, Captain Bond, wearing swim trunks and no diving lung.

Bond had made a record, free ascent from more than 320 feet wearing only a face mask and life vest and he believed that, with a hood and by breathing mixed gases like helium instead of air, ascent could be made from considerably greater depths. But Bond's relatively simple escape mechanism would not be usable at the operating depths of nuclear submarines. For this reason he began a search for safer means for rescuing men from these depths.

In 1957 at the Navy's submarine school at New London, Dr. George Bond and his associates began experiments in which they exposed animals to deep pressures for long periods. They breathed a special helium-oxygen mix. Eventually Captain Bond and his team were able to keep goats at a 200-foot pressure for two weeks at a time. Navy requirements interrupted this important research work, so Bond had to yield his efforts temporarily to Edwin Link and Robert Stenuit.

In April 1963 Bond successfully held three men for six days at a pressure of 100 feet in a laboratory experiment and, in September 1963, he ran a test with three volunteers exposed to pressures equivalent to 200-feet of water for 12 days without any apparent harmful effects. Bond was now ready to begin operational testing on the sea floor.

On July 18, 1964, preparations were completed for the first Navy undersea station, *Sealab I*. It had taken Bond five years to get official approval and the funds to build his underwater research laboratory. Bond's cylindrical steel capsule was lowered 192 feet to its underwater resting place at Plantagenet Bank—26 miles southwest of Bermuda near the Navy's oceanographic research tower, Argus Island. Four Navy divers descended to take up housekeeping two days later. The pressure inside the capsule was kept at 86 pounds per square inch which was equal to that of the surrounding ocean. The men breathed a mixture of 80 percent helium, 4 percent oxygen and 16 percent nitrogen. The resulting thin air made their voices high-pitched giving a Mickey Mouse effect whenever they tried to talk. After two days of listening, they were able to understand each other. The aquanauts also found that they became so sleepy after meals that they were forced to take a nap to regain their energy.

Originally Astronaut Carpenter was to have participated in this experiment but a last minute mishap on land prevented his going. The four-man aquanaut team that made the dive included a doctor, Lt. Commander Robert E. Thompson of the Navy Medical Corps. The aquanauts had a two-man baby sub, *Star I*, and a full-sized submarine in their front yard for company.

After ten days of the planned three-week *Sealab I* experiment had been completed, gale warnings forced Bond to bring the men up prematurely. Despite this unfortunate abbreviation of the experiment, the initial trial was felt to be a success. Commander Thompson carried out exhaustive medical tests on himself and his colleagues during the ten-day stay below. Each man swam out in the surrounding water to perform research chores for an average of four hours a day. The outside of the *Sealab I* was rigged with stationary flash cameras triggered from the surface whenever the TV monitor on the mothership showed something interesting below.

A year later Bond received $1,800,000 from the Office of Naval Research to underwrite a more sophisticated *Sealab II* experiment in the Pacific. He corralled 28 volunteers — including astronaut turned aquanaut, Commander M. Scott Carpenter —to take part in his newest project.

Carpenter, one of the seven original Mercury astronauts, was born in Boulder, Colorado, on May 1, 1925. After graduating from the University of Colorado he joined the Navy for flight training. He flew patrol missions in the Korean conflict and served as a Navy test pilot until his selection as an astronaut in 1959. Scott Carpenter made his historic space flight in the Mercury capsule *Aurora 7* on May 24, 1962. Three years later he was given the privilege of exploring the other frontier. Before making his first sea plunge Commander Carpenter made an observation on the similarities between the two environments. "I understand," he said, "there is some euphoria under water, . . . there is some in space flight too."

Carpenter, who had already become a new type of American folk-hero as an astronaut, lent some good publicity and glamour to the man-in-the-sea experiment. His presence helped to underline the importance and better understanding of the program after it was made clear that his participation was not just a "gimmick" or publicity stunt. When he finally made his descent in *Sealab II* in 1965, Carpenter became the first human to experience the two most hostile environments known.

On August 28 the first team of nine aquanauts led by Carpenter descended 205 feet to the sea floor to take up residence in their 12- by 58-foot steel cylin-

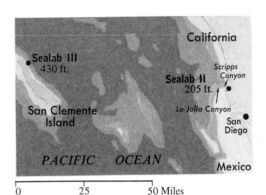

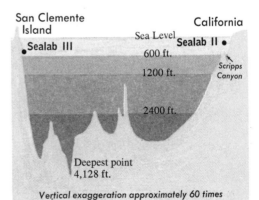

Sealab II was lowered 205 feet into Scripps Canyon in 1965. Sealab III is scheduled to descend 430 feet off San Clemente Island.

der. As Carpenter and his nine fellow aquanauts settled down to work deep below the surface of the Pacific, they started to make daily "reconnaissance sorties" outside of their underwater barracks. Their first task outside of the *Sealab II* was to hook up bright lights outside their submerged home to illuminate the surrounding depths.

Later they connected cables from the *Sealab* to a seven-ton, beehive-shaped laboratory containing a multi-channeled television and telephone station that provided the primary communications between the underwater base and the twin-hulled barge floating overhead that served as a mother-ship. Each day the men left their underwater home to perform tasks in 47- to 50-degree water outside. They mapped the ocean floor and studied local marine life and made exploratory dives to depths of 300 feet in Scripps Canyon.

Leaving the submerged *Sealab* vessel was "about as easy as falling off a log," according to the aquanauts who could leave the *Sealab* either via one of two floor hatches or a top exit in a conning tower. The atmospheric pressure in the *Sealab* was kept at 100 pounds per square inch to keep the ocean water from rushing in. Below the main hatch was a wire mesh cage with a door to protect the residents from possible attacks by sharks during the vulnerable period of entering or leaving the *Sealab*.

One day, soon after the program got underway, the aquanauts were paid a visit by a non-human mammal. Tuffy, a trained seven-foot porpoise, joined the U.S. Navy's man-in-the-sea program. He did not stay with the divers but acted as their liaison courier with the surface. Tuffy wore a plastic harness and carried mail wrapped in a waterproof tube to the aquanauts. He also took tools to divers and, when one diver pretended to be lost in the murky water with a visibility of ten feet, Tuffy swam 50 feet to him with a nylon lifeline to lead him back to the *Sealab*.

Aboard the support vessel Bond and his other medical assistants kept a close watch on the mental and physical well-being of the divers. Samples of blood, saliva and urine of each aquanaut were sent topside each day along with checks on their blood pressure and brain waves as they worked, ate and slept below. To guard against panic by any of the aquanauts from the cold and darkness, Bond saw to it that his men worked in pairs and used lifelines connected to the capsule. Each aquanaut was also equipped to receive an acoustical beacon that would guide him back in the murky darkness if his line was accidentally severed.

The monitoring of the conversations between the aquanauts in the capsule and the oceanographic scientists aboard the mother-ship disclosed that most of the men were suffering considerable hardships. Nine of the ten found themselves afflicted with skin rashes and painful ear infections but none so painful that they had to come up to the surface prematurely. Some of the protective, rubberized "wet suits" were found to be inadequate, which resulted in paralyzing coldness and forced the men to abandon their experiments outside the capsule and return earlier than planned to the relative warmth of the *Sealab*.

In the *Sealab I* experiment in 1964, the work curve of the four aquanauts had plunged sharply below their normal performance. But the *Sealab II* aquanauts showed outstanding performances, which Bond explained resulted from their superior physical conditioning before their descent, coupled with the higher morale stemming from the presence of a larger team (over double the size of the original one) and changes in the capsule's atmosphere.

As the first nine aquanauts prepared to leave the *Sealab* at the end of their 15-day stay, Carpenter was stung by the dorsal spines of a red scorpion fish. Carpenter's injury was treated with painkilling drugs and cortisone. After an hour's treatment,

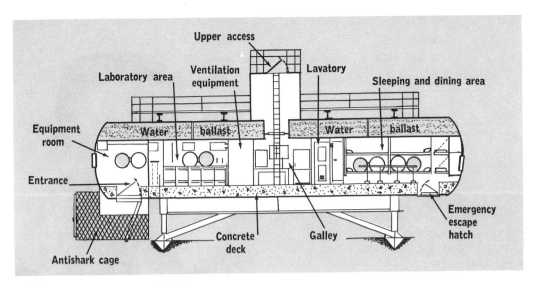

Upper access

Ventilation
equipment

Lavatory

Laboratory area

Sleeping and dining area

Equipment
room

Water   ballast

Water   ballast

Entrance

Emergency
escape
hatch

Antishark cage

Concrete
deck

Galley

Cross section of the 38-foot Sealab II.

it was decided that he was responding well enough to complete his 30-day stay. The other nine aquanauts returned to the surface in a pressurized transfer tank and the second team of aquanauts took up residence in *Sealab II*.

After a record 30 days spent on the Pacific's floor, Carpenter ascended to the surface and the last team of divers began the final segment of the experiment. Carpenter told a news conference two days later of the beauty, pain and hard manual labor that he and his fellow aquanauts experienced below. "The ocean is a much more hostile environment than space," he said. "I worked harder in *Sealab II* than in the Mercury capsule. More energy is required just to move around, because of the extreme pressure, and just to stay warm, because of the 50-degree cold."

"But the real key," he concluded, "is the isolation. I think men can live as long in underwater habitats as they can in DEW line stations or any place elsewhere they are isolated. I am convinced that men can live and work any length of time they wish beneath the surface of the ocean."

At the conclusion of the *Sealab II* experiment Captain Bond said the three teams had successfully accomplished more than 200 man-hours of work outside despite the cold and murky water. He and his associates said the experience of the

divers showed a need for heated diving suits and the redesigning of future underwater huts.

Bond felt that the men had performed their tasks so satisfactorily that he could envision a time when men could live indefinitely in underwater capsules while performing extended work deep on the ocean floor. But Lt. Robert E. Sonnenburg, a Navy doctor who lived in the capsule with two of the three aquanaut teams, countered this optimistic prediction by noting that the efficiency of the men who lived in *Sealab II* had declined significantly as a result of various ailments that appeared. Yet Bond felt that these ailments could be overcome in time with proper medication, clothing and precautions.

An improved underwater station, *Sealab III*, is scheduled to make its descent 430 feet into Pacific waters off San Clemente Island in late 1968. The Navy's man-in-the-sea program, directed by George Bond, is expected to continue until aquanauts have lived for a month or more at depths of 850 feet. Experiments in undersea living at such depths will put us well within reach of the continental shelves. The first perilous steps into the new frontier have been taken. For Bond and Carpenter there are no doubts about the potential rewards if we give our ocean efforts support comparable to our efforts in space.

Willard Bascom

Willard Bascom is a 51-year-old mining engineer who can be called a kind of modern-day Christopher Columbus. But unlike the Italian mariner who opened up the New World by sailing across the seas horizontally, Bascom is leading the way for the coming vertical exploitation of the oceans and the sea bottom — for both wealth and knowledge.

His new firm, Ocean Science and Engineering Inc., has already staked out claims to thousands of square miles of potentially valuable sea bottom all over the world in the hopes of hauling out millions of dollars worth of gold, diamonds,

tin and other valuable metals from the ocean depths. He is also concerned with the design and manufacturing of ships and machines to explore and understand the sea.

Bascom, the president and founder of his unique firm, is a multi-talented individual, being an inventor, engineer, hard-rock miner, writer, moviemaker and mariner who can double either as gang boss on a project or company president. As head of one company among many which hope to mine the sea, Bascom realizes that he has to keep several paces ahead of the larger, well-established firms such as

Standard Oil, General Dynamics, Lockheed, and Reynolds Metals which also see a huge potential profit on the wet frontier. But unlike these other corporations, which have a peripheral interest in the oceans, Bascom and his associates concern themselves only with the sea.

His firm offers to work "anywhere in the oceans on any kind of a problem." Ocean Science and Engineering Inc. is prepared to cope with tides, storms, and battering waves in the pursuit of its stated mission. Bascom sees the ocean not only as a source of minerals but as potential industrial sites. His company has already designed an undersea nuclear power plant to be built off the coast of Point Arguello, California, where it will be surrounded by limitless supplies of cooling water.

Bascom and his four chief associates pioneered the ill-fated Mohole Project, which was a national undertaking to drill through the ocean floor several miles down and sample the earth's deep interior. Bascom describes this unique undertaking in his book, *A Hole In The Bottom Of The Sea.* He conceived the original ship positioning equipment that made the whole massive undertaking practical and in a 1961 test off lower California put a string of drill pipes two miles down to the floor of the Pacific and brought up rock cores from beneath the sandy, muddy bottom.

In addition to the Mohole Project which skyrocketed Bascom to the forefront of today's cadre of topflight ocean engineers, his firm built the prospecting ship *Rockeater* to search for undersea diamonds off Southwest Africa for the great De Beers diamond mining syndicate. OS&E has also built a submersible with television eyes that can spot spent torpedoes or sunken ships 6,000 feet below the surface in addition to building a system for inspecting the deep Atlantic cables for Bell Telephone Co.

Bascom is a good-looking, youthful man with premature graying hair. A maverick for most of his life and disillusioned by age 40 with more prosaic ways of making a living, he took his wife and daughter to Tahiti in 1957 and spent the next 19 months at leisure, reading under the palm trees. When his money ran out he toyed with the idea of moving on to New Zealand but decided at the last minute to give up his gypsy life and come back to the United States. He has been deeply immersed in various ocean engineering projects all over the world ever since.

Bascom was born in the upper middle class suburb of Bronxville in Westchester County, New York, where his mother ran a nursery school. After graduating from high school, where he built up a reputation as a brilliant but erratic student, young Bascom enrolled at Springfield College in Massachusetts but quit after his first year.

Returning home, he landed a job on a construction project helping to build an aqueduct linking the New York City water system with a Catskill Mountain reservoir. On this tough job he learned to handle a pneumatic drill and twice escaped death in cave-ins because he had luckily swapped shifts with other men. But after three years on this sweaty job, he finally became aware that a mine boss needed more education than he could get working underground. So at age 21, with $500 donated by one of his mother's wealthy neighbors to stake him to a restart in his educational career, he left New York in 1938 and enrolled in the Colorado School of Mines.

He was an honor student from the beginning but did not get along well with some of his professors and the college authorities. In 1942, just before his graduation, he got into a sticky row with a geology professor whose reasoning he found faulty. The President of the college asked Bascom to apologize but the professor refused to listen. As a result an enraged Bascom walked out and left the campus without receiving his degree.

He then moved on to the western mining camps where he filled odd jobs as a shift boss, civil engineer and timber man. He worked his way from the Arizona Rockies to Washington's Olympic Mountains, and by 1945 he bumped into a University of California scientist, John Isaacs, who asked him to spend a few weeks on a study of Pacific Coast beaches. Bascom agreed to help out on the project without understanding what it all meant. Soon he discovered that the knowledge gained from the wave study would become the key to plans for the coming invasion of Japan. This was important because almost nothing was known of the offshore contours of the beaches upon which American troops would have landed if the two atomic bombs dropped on Hiroshima and Nagasaki had not ended the war.

He ended up running the beach project and clearly demonstrated that beach contours could be predicted from the way waves behaved when they felt the bottom and then crested. The entire project took five years with Bascom working in the surf from Mexico to Canada using clumsy looking amphibious DUKWS. His full report, published in 1950 as a five-volume work, entitled *A Shoreline Atlas of the Pacific Coast,* is still labeled "Top Secret" since it was in reality a key to the invasion of the western United States. (Bascom has not even been allowed to possess a copy for himself.)

Bascom had intended to return to mining when he completed the study, but he discovered that his attitudes and ambitions had changed during the course of his work on the waves and the beaches. He became an early scuba diver addict and was instrumental in the invention of the neoprene, foam-rubber "wet suit"—which is now standard equipment for most scuba divers. He also invented a diver-to-surface communications system which used a sonar beam for voice transmission.

In 1951 he went to Eniwetok to measure waves stirred up by our nuclear testing and while there invented the taut-moored buoy. By shortening the anchor line which pulled the buoy beneath the waves and making the cable rigid, Bascom was able to achieve a stable platform for his recorders and remain on station instead of drifting with the tides and the winds.

All of his unique oceanographic inventions were mere by-products, however, of the intellectual broadening wrought by the challenge of his new environment. Unfortunately, just as he began to embark on a new phase in his career, he found that he had cancer. In 1951 a malignant growth was discovered which cut off the circulation to his left leg. When he began falling down on the sidewalk, he sought medical help. Bascom was told he would have to face amputation. He rejected the surgeon's diagnosis and was proved right when massive radiation recommended by another medical doctor cured him. Two later growths were also eradicated by the same means, and he has had no recurrence during the past decade. Meanwhile Bascom had become interested in the Mohole Project, a mammoth gamble to try and pierce the earth's crust beneath the sea.

A half century earlier, the Croatian seismologist, Dr. Andrija Mohorovicic, had discovered that shock waves of the 1909 earthquake traveled more rapidly through the rock beneath the earth's crust than through the rock on the earth's surface. The European scientist hypothesized that there was a discernible demarcation line or discontinuity dividing the two layers. This boundary between crust and mantle was later named the Mohorovicic Discontinuity, or "Moho," in his honor. Science has speculated ever since about the temperature, composition, magnetic and radioactive qualities of the material below the Moho.

The quest for answers to these questions led two scientists in 1957 to the wild suggestion that someone drill through the Moho and bring up a sample of the earth's mantle. Since the earth's crust is thinnest under the oceans, the best place to attempt such a drill hole might be mid-ocean.

The idea was unveiled at a wine breakfast held at the California home of geophysicist Walter Munk, who was a member of the American Miscellaneous Society. This semi-ludicrous, informal organization, known popularly by its initials-AMSOC, had been conceived in parody of the more pompous American scientific bodies. Munk invited some fellow members of the Society to his La Jolla home to consider his and Princeton geologist Harry Hess' suggestion for a deep-sea drilling to the mantle.

Happily Munk discovered that the members present were delighted with the idea despite some grave doubts rendered about the project's practicality. Since the deepest oil well on earth in the year 1957 had only gone down to 22,570 feet in Louisiana, there was still some serious question as to whether the Moho could be reached because it was at least one-third again deeper.

Furthermore it was known that no hole of any kind had ever been drilled beneath more than a few hundred feet of sea. This knowledge was coupled with the fact that there was no known drilling platform capable of staying on station offshore. Despite these known difficulties, AMSOC made a formal proposal to the National Science Foundation the next year and received a modest $15,000 grant to conduct a "feasibility study."

Although this didn't seem like a great sum of money, it pleased Bascom who was asked to conduct the study. He was electrified by the possibilities. "I might have spent my whole life training for that one thing," he said as he plunged into a self-administered six-months' cram course in geophysics. After coining the word "Mohole" and writing an article for *Scientific American* on the project, he was happy to discover that the National Science Foundation now had enough faith in him and the

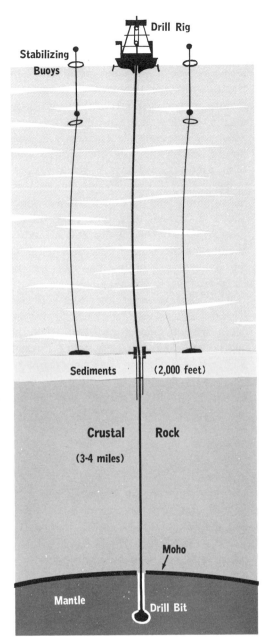

Drilling through the sediments and crustal rock below the oceans to bring up samples of the underlying mantle is the dream of scientists.

project to up the ante to $1.5 million for a "hardware test" of deep-sea drilling techniques.

To accomplish the first phase of this tremendous task, Bascom chartered a big, oil-drilling ship called *Cuss I*. It previously had been operated only inshore and at anchor. To keep this cumbersome vessel in one spot on the ocean, Bascom invented a new system of "dynamic positioning" by placing four giant, diesel-powered outboard motors at each corner of the rig and coordinating them with a central control lever. Then, by operating the engines in opposition to one another with the help of some of his taut-moored buoys, Bascom was able to keep *Cuss I* from straying more than half a ship's length despite 20-knot winds and 15-foot high seas. The pipe did not hang straight but was subject to a kind of bending as the *Cuss I* rose and fell with the motions of the waves—like Charlie Chaplin's cane in the old silent movies.

After sinking some test holes off San Diego, Bascom took the *Cuss I* to a deep-ocean area off Guadalupe Island where he and his oilfield roughnecks drilled through 560 feet of gray-green Miocene ooze lying under two miles of water. At the end of the 20th day they struck a layer of basalt below the mud and triumphantly brought up some rock core samples. The experimental drilling was a success.

When they returned to port they were acclaimed for their feat, receiving a personal compliment from President Kennedy, as well as a hero's welcome by AMSOC and the rest of the scientific community. The National Science Foundation felt that the administration of the project should now be moved under the umbrella of a larger, private contractor. After the proposals of 12 competing firms were evaluated, it was concluded that the Socony-Mobil Oil Company was in a "class by itself." Bascom, who had been assured continued direction of the project, was delighted by the prospect of working with such a cooperative ally. But then politics entered the picture. Brown and Root, an influential Texas construction firm, was raised from fifth to first place in the bidding and got the coveted contract. Brown and Root spent almost $40 million of government funds to build a fancy Mohole drilling platform which was never completed. Congress, discouraged by the snail-like progress, cut off all Mohole appropriations in 1966.

Although Bascom felt a sense of regret at the apparent death of his project, he did not let the political and technical doldrums of the Mohole cloud his vision. His initial bitterness was soon overcome by new prospects on the horizon. He and his four original associates, who started Ocean Science and Engineering with a meager $9,500 in capital, were gratified to see the stock in the firm rise to $4.5 million.

Several major firms bought up to 10 percent of Ocean Science's stock as his business boomed to over $3 million in sales in 1965. Bascom and OS&E Inc. had finally arrived in the big time with its busy president and founder wearing four hats at once; chief administrator, salesman, publicist and promotion manager. His recent financial success after all the previous lean years has strengthened Bascom's conviction that the ocean bottom should be mined right now. In late 1966 and 1967 his firm explored 8,000 square miles of tin-bearing sands off Tasmania. They acquired rights to 7,000 more square miles of ocean bottom off the Philippines where they hope to mine gold and chromite. They are also involved in mining operations of tin and gems off Malaya and Thailand. Bascom's firm is currently prospecting for gold in the frigid offshore waters of Alaska.

In September 1967 the JOIDES deep-sea drilling project was announced in which some 50 holes are to be drilled under the Atlantic and Pacific Oceans. It will attempt to salvage the remnants of the ill-fated Mohole Project using Bascom's dynamic positioning techniques. Scientists hope to get sufficient evidence to piece together the history of the ocean basins and test recent theories on ocean-floor spreading. One way or another, Bascom and his associate oceanographers are determined to probe ever deeper into the seabeds to unlock the secrets of the earth. Maybe Project Mohole is not dead after all.

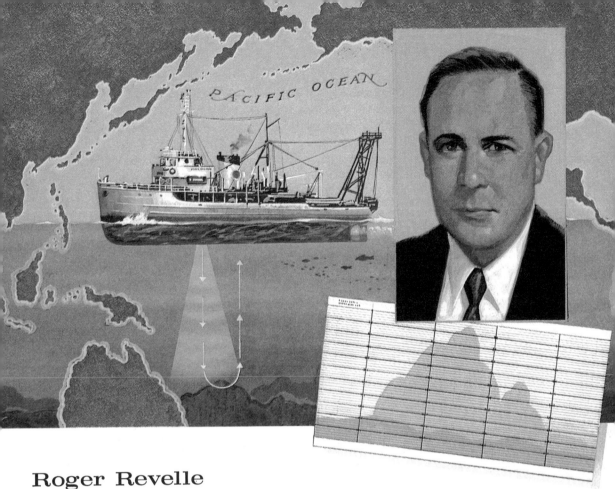

Roger Revelle

Roger Randall Dougan Revelle, one of our outstanding contemporary oceanographers, is a man whose interests are easily broad enough to encompass the seven seas and the people who live on all the continents they surround. For this reason, in 1964, he easily shifted from the position of administrating one of our leading scientific marine research centers, the Scripps Institution of Oceanography in California, and moved east to Harvard University to take over a new and challenging post in order to try to discover how to cope with the growing problem of too many people.

In his new position at the Center for Population Studies, he soon came to realize that mastering the new space and marine technologies would not be enough; that men and nations had to learn also how to get along more compatibly if the fruits of these new scientific advances were to be put to mankind's use and advantage.

Revelle is truly an "oceanographer's oceanographer" — who has helped to integrate successfully geography, geology, geophysics and meteorology into a mature and sophisticated marine science that could take its place proudly with the older sciences. Dr. Revelle's own humorous definition of oceanographers is: "They are sailors who use big words."

He has built up a reputation for bulling things through, and has been known to act so vigorously and stubbornly on behalf of his favorite causes that he often evoked acrimony from his opponents. The six-foot, four-inch-tall Revelle has been described as "a man who looks as if he were specially designed, both physically and temperamentally to study the Pacific Ocean."

This handsome, square-jawed man has been known to work to the point of exhaustion, following a tight dawn-to-dusk schedule that is reminiscent of a whirlwind.

Revelle has been devoted to oceanography in all its phases ever since 1929. But in more recent years, he has been concerned with international projects which sharpened his interest in problems that bore on the current "explosion" in human population.

Chief among these was the study and report on the Indus Valley undertaken by a panel of American experts; hydrologists, engineers and agronomists, headed by Revelle. The study was made at the request of the Government of Pakistan. Revelle was then serving as science advisor to the Secretary of the Interior. While holding important positions with the University of California he has headed other such projects over the years, reflecting his concern for international problems.

He was Dean of Research at California with university-wide responsibilities when he was selected for the Harvard post. But his most lasting career impact was made during the three and a half decades that he was associated with the Scripps Institution of Oceanography at La Jolla, where he served as director from 1951 to 1964. In the early sixties, he helped to expand the university's units at La Jolla and San Diego into major campuses of the university system. His campaign for expansion of the university caused resentment within certain university circles as did his vigorous opposition to the administrative establishment and compulsory loyalty oaths for members of the faculty. This may have led to his being bypassed for the post of university chancellor of the new La Jolla campus.

Revelle was born in Seattle, Washington, on March 7, 1909. He was enrolled in Pomona College in lower California in the humanities curriculum and was active on student publications until a professor aroused his interest in science. He switched his major to geology which he pursued through a year of graduate work at Claremont in 1929-30. Then he moved to the prestigious University of California

where he stumbled into the field of oceanography.

After the university's oceanographic yacht, *Carnegie*, blew up by accident at Numea in the South Pacific, some of the salvaged ocean-bottom cores that its scientists had obtained were returned to the Scripps Institution for study. Revelle, now a full-fledged geologist, was sent down the coast from Berkeley to analyze them. "Then the first thing I knew," he reminisced later, "they had me going to sea on expeditions. I said: 'This is wonderful—you work and take boat trips at the same time'—so I stayed there." During the next several years he worked on his doctorate at Scripps, serving as a teaching-assistant to pay for his tuition.

In 1931, Revelle married Ellen Clark, a student in the first graduating class at Scripps College, which was endowed by her great-aunt, Ellen Browning Scripps. By 1941, Revelle had risen to the rank of assistant professor at Scripps. During World War II, he served in the Navy in a scientific capacity at the Hydrographic Office in Washington, as the officer-in-charge of the Oceanographic Section of the Bureau of Ships where he was able to keep up his marine research. After the war, Revelle was involved in classified work for the Navy at the Eniwetok and Bikini nuclear bomb tests in 1946 and 1947.

In 1951, after serving for two decades on the staff of Scripps, he was appointed the director of that esteemed world's largest oceanographic institution—the first alumnus to be appointed to the post. During the next few years, he conducted several noteworthy oceanographic expeditions into the Pacific Ocean and wrote several articles about his findings. The motivating force behind these various expeditions was Revelle's concern that "only about two percent of the sea floor has been even moderately surveyed. As far as our understanding of the topography of the sea floor is concerned, we are now about

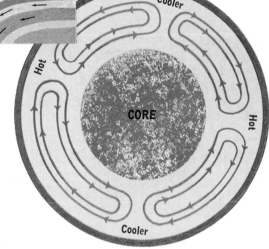

The Tonga Trench, a 35,000-foot chasm, is thought to have been formed from downward movements in the earth's crust.

Convection currents, deep within the mantle, may account for changes in the earth's crust.

where we were a hundred years ago in surveying the land."

In the 1950's Revelle led oceanographic expeditions to the Central and Southwest Pacific. During surveys of the Tonga Trench area Revelle's team of researchers came up with significant geophysical data that has helped to change earlier concepts of the ocean basins as "permanent" unchanging features. Besides obtaining an echo sounding of 5,814 fathoms (a record depth for that part of the Pacific), they recorded surprisingly low heat flow and gravity acceleration values in trench areas. They also found evidence of horizontal movement of the ocean floor and gradual deepening of the trench itself. Studies by Ewing and others have found high heat-flow values and gravity anomalies along the axis of mid-ocean ridges.

Revelle points out that some of the phenomena observed can be explained by a single hypothesis which sees great convection currents in the earth's mantle. The ridges can by viewed as regions of upward-migrating, hot mantle rocks and the trenches as areas where the crust is being pulled down into the earth by downward-flowing currents in the cooler parts of the mantle. Revelle cites the evidence of fossil clams, sea urchins that have been found on seamounts thousands of feet below sea level, as an indication of possible submergence of ancient ridge areas due to the pulling-down process. Convection in the mantle may also have released water from the earth's interior, thus increasing the volume of water, and may have con-

tributed to the drowning of seamounts and coral atolls.

As head of Scripps Institution, Revelle did not let his personal interest in marine geology overshadow investigations in other phases of oceanography. When, in December 1954, Revelle and Scripps received $1 million from the Rockefeller Fund to expand their ocean resources research programs, Revelle commented: "In some respects marine biology has lagged behind the other biological sciences. Because of advances in other fields, notably in genetics and chemistry, many problems are now ripe for solution. Life began in the sea and from the sea we may learn something about life's basic processes."

It is ironical that, although the oceans cover 70 percent of the earth's surface, they are utilized to supply only one percent of man's food, despite the increasing food shortage. Revelle is aware that before more effective fishing techniques and apparatus can be developed, there must be a thorough

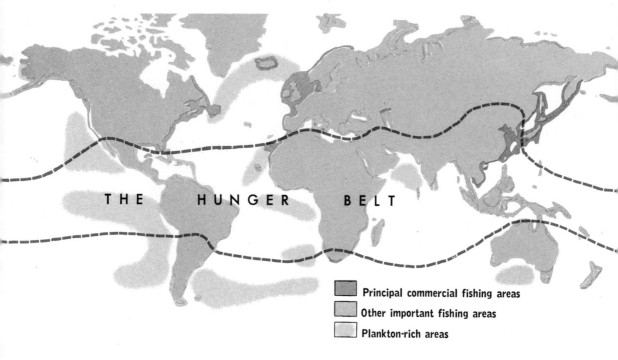

THE HUNGER BELT

Principal commercial fishing areas
Other important fishing areas
Plankton-rich areas

Most of the world's main fishing grounds lie outside the densely populated "Hunger Belt."

understanding of the relationships of marine animals to their ocean environment and to each other. Men must first know the processes that make some parts of the ocean fertile pastures and others sterile deserts. Systematic study of the ecology of marine plants and the whole "food chain" must precede any hopes of increasing our harvest of the sea's living resources.

As a result of his marine researches over the years, Revelle received the coveted Agassiz medal in 1963 from the National Academy of Sciences for his outstanding contributions to oceanography. In the summer of 1964, just before taking over his new post at Harvard in the fall, Revelle chaired an *ad hoc* study panel of the Special Committee on Ocean Research (SCOR) of the International Council of Scientific Unions, which put together a "general scientific framework for world ocean study." In their interesting paper, the panel wrote an important document to arouse interest in mining the oceans, to stimulate thinking among oceanographers,

and to examine the economic benefits that might result from a greater knowledge of the sea. The opening sentence of their report is intriguing: "Seawater contains many of the minerals necessary to the world's chemical industry, yet there never has been a venturesome and vigorous evaluation of its potential mineral resources. The panel then went on to ask open-end questions about the possibilities of extracting magnesium, cesium, copper, rubidum and other minerals from the sea.

After Harvard scoured the country for a year and a half, seeking an outstanding person to head their new Center for Population Studies at the School of Public Health they finally chose Revelle for the task. For those who were surprised at an oceanographer being picked for the post, the rationale made sense since life began in the oceans and life on earth is still dependent on them. Dr. Nathan Pusey, the President of Harvard, in announcing Revelle's appointment, said candidly: "He is a scientific administrator of broad experience and great talent, extraordinarily qualified to organize and lead the joint attack which members of the new Center for Population Studies will make on the complex problems arising from the imbalance between numbers of people in the world and the means to sustain them in health and well-being."

Since the problem of global overpopulation has been judged by most political and economic experts as having become the primary challenge to mankind for the rest of the century, Revelle has found himself in a crucial post. Increasing present yield of human protein food from the sea would be only a partial solution. To achieve a balance between population and resources will require more than a spurt in marine research and technology to increase the yield of the sea. It involves attacking all sorts of problems in a number of different fields—social sciences, economics, sociology, anthropology and education—to name just a few. Time is running out and the need for broad, comprehensive research and planning is all too critical to permit longer delay.

In his poetic introduction to the excellent popular book on oceanography, *Frontiers of the Sea*, authored by Robert Cowen in 1960, Revelle summed up his philosophical approach to his lifetime career, which could easily be adapted as a guide for future oceanographers: "It is an ironic fact," he wrote, "that we are learning to leave this planet just when we are beginning to think about it as a whole, as our planetary home. With our Sputniks and Explorers, our deep space probes and Project Mercuries, we shall soon soar beyond all horizons. But men were never as aware as they are today that their survival depends on careful husbanding of every resource on Earth. This realization has led to a great surge of interest in the largest and least known feature of the Earth's surface, the ocean . . .

"Men like ourselves have lived on Earth for perhaps five hundred thousand years, yet through all but a tiny fraction of that time our ancestors might have been bacteria proliferating on the skin of an orange, for all they knew about their world. Only within the last few centuries have men had sufficient understanding to be able to think of the Earth as a whole, as a sphere unsupported in space, isolated and complete in itself, yet held in its appointed place by describable though invisible forces . . ."

Then Revelle went on to postulate why oceanographers have an important role to play in helping us to understand the bulk of the sphere on which we live. He wrote: "Oceanographers are not such a serious-minded lot that they keep asking themselves why they are doing their job. The spiritual ancestor of most of them was Ulysses. He was called the Wanderer, because he was the first to venture into the River Ocean, out of the salt and fishy Sea-between-the-Land, the wine-dark Mediterranean. Perhaps he disliked administration, hated farming, and was bored by Penelope. In any case, Ulysses managed to spend a great deal of time away from home. He never stated his reasons very clearly, but he still lives in the hearts of oceanographers, the scientists who go to sea."

These lines of Alfred Lord Tennyson seem to sum up Revelle's philosophy—

There lies the port; the vessel puffs her
    sail:
There gloom the dark, broad seas. My
    mariners . . .
That ever with a frolic welcome took
The thunder and the sunshine . . . Come
    my friends . . .
Push off, and sitting well in order smite
The sounding furrows; for my purpose
    holds
To sail beyond the sunset, and the baths
Of all the western stars . . .
Some work of noble note, may yet be
    done . . .

Oceanographers like sailors have "work of noble note" to do.

Man's Future Beneath the Sea

Man has only two vast, natural frontiers left to him: outer space and the oceans, both of which are still virtually unexplored and unexploited. In the years to come, technological breakthroughs will make possible a major escalation on the part of the world's oceanographers to develop the resources of the oceans for the benefit of mankind. The new realm of hydrospace will provide thousands of new job opportunities and bring about the birth of dozens of new industries as our oceanic engineers perfect the techniques to dive deeper and stay longer under the surface of the seas.

Some of the new marine industries which are either still unborn or just getting started include: fish farming; underwater agriculture, including the direct consumption of plankton; utilizing the power of the sea in such tidal projects as Passamaquoddy and the Bay of Fundy off Nova Scotia; the development of new medicines and antibiotics from marine life; the transportation of passengers and cargo in commercial nuclear-powered submarines; the growth of large scale underseas mining of oil and minerals such as gold and manganese; and other related practical applications of marine technology.

On the more exotic level we can now foresee the eventual development of liquid-breathing devices so that the aquanauts of the future can dispense with their air tanks and breathe water directly into the lungs through artificial gills; the construction of underwater recreation areas, hotels, cities and submerged naval bases; and the training of porpoises to do man's bidding and help him to exploit the potentials of the deep. These are but a few of the more fascinating types of projects looming on the horizon.

In fishing technology, the Russians and the Japanese lead the world in the perfection of techniques of attracting fish with an electric field as a replacement for the age-old methods of hook and line and nets. While the United States has taken a back seat in this area, it is hoped that our marine scientists will be able to improve upon recent innovations in finding fish and catching them. The present Russian and Japanese automated factory-ships and fishing fleets can stay at sea for months, preparing everything from fillets to fish meal, or from cod liver oil to canned sardines, with the additional capability of freezing the rest of their catches.

But we cannot increase the productivity of the sea until our oceanic engineers and scientists obtain more knowledge about the complex interrelations among the organisms of the marine community. With proper cultivation the world's fish catch might be doubled or tripled by the end of the century. More importantly, the possibilities of aquaculture offer additional opportunities for feeding an exploding global population in the years to come. The Japanese have already developed productive and efficient sea-farming of shrimp and oysters and the Dutch have transplanted mussels from their original beds to richer waters for fattening and eventual harvest.

Those who accept the responsibility for planning the mass exploitation of the oceans for the benefit of man in tomorrow's world will have to use caution, however, and not attempt to accelerate the changes in the lives of marine organisms at too fast a rate. Otherwise, we might accomplish more harm than good by killing off whole species or polluting the sea to the point where we will have created a lifeless desert under water.

The new awareness of ocean potential has wrought some important shifts in our Government's approach to gearing the nation for a major oceanographic effort. Within the past few years, several organizational reshuffles have occurred in the Department of Commerce, the principal branch of the Government having jurisdiction over our civilian oceanographic efforts; in the Navy Department; and in Congress, where two acts of legislation were passed concerning the organization of our national oceanographic efforts and the education of oceanographers. Each of these steps appears to be rather insignificant by itself, but when looked upon as a whole they add up to a significant move forward for the nation.

The first step occurred when Dr. Harris Stewart, the former Chief Oceanographer of the Coast and Geodetic Survey, was picked to head the new Institute of Oceanography in the Environmental Science Services Administration under the Department of Commerce on December 25, 1965. After his appointment as director of this new agency, he commented: "It shows the increasing emphasis on the importance of research in this field. We hope to fill the gap between basic research at the private oceanographic institutes and the people who are physically pounding on the doors now for environmental information about the oceans that can be put to immediate, practical use."

Then in June 1966, President Johnson signed into law the Marine Resources and Engineering Development Act which marked the first national legislation ever to be passed by Congress, recognizing

By flooding her stern, FLIP (Floating Instrument Platform) becomes a stable, vertical research laboratory. This Scripps research vessel must be towed to and from location.

the importance of oceanology and oceanography. At the heart of the bill, sponsored by Senator Warren Magnuson of Washington, was a provision for the appointment of a 15-member study commission made up of selected government, industry, university and marine laboratory figures.

Since the Russians recognized the need for a major national effort in the marine sciences years before we did, as evidenced by their larger fleet consisting of over 120 oceanographic vessels, the legislation did not come any too soon. The hope is that eventually this bill will do for our country what the space act did in 1958—effectively advance the status of the United States as a leader in marine science.

The Navy issued its own recommendation for exploiting the wet frontier by calling for a rapid expansion of ocean research that could mount to $1 billion a year by 1970. Such a program, stressing the exploitation of the new deep-sea technological capability of this country, could do much to help us re-establish our position in the race for utilization of the seas.

These organizational moves are reminiscent of our post-Sputnik panic which occurred almost a decade earlier when we created NASA to direct our space efforts. Now we are presently faced with the knowledge that the Soviet Union is far ahead of us in the race for inner space with its recently expanded oceanographic program based on an apparent belief that underseas exploration can lead to control of the world. By mid-1968 the Soviets had a two-to-one margin in marine scientists and three-to-one in oceanographic engineers to exploit the ocean frontier. This is a sad commentary on America's current lag in so vital an area. It does not properly reflect our proud, but often overlooked, heritage of quality in this field.

A decade ago, only 26 American universities offered courses in oceanography. Today there are 66 such schools, a threefold increase. According to the reports from the National Science Foundation and the Interagency Committee on Oceanography, we need some 6,000 new oceanographers by 1972. There are not enough graduates to fill the growing demand.

In the fall of 1966, after becoming aware of the shortage, Congress passed the first sea-grant college bill which marked the first national legislation ever enacted to support the education and training of American marine scientists and technicians. This new $30 million program, spread over a three-year period, was patterned after the Land-Grant College Act of the mid-19th century.

In mid-1966, Lyndon B. Johnson proposed a radical approach to the future exploitation of the oceans.

"Under no circumstances, we believe, must we ever allow the prospects of rich harvest and mineral wealth to create a new form of colonial competition among the maritime nations. We must be careful to avoid a race to grab and to hold the lands under the high seas. We must ensure that the deep seas and the ocean bottom are, and remain, the legacy of all human beings."

These words, uttered by President Johnson on July 13, 1966, at the dedication of the new U.S. marine research vessel, the 3,800-ton *Oceanographer,** may be among the most significant of his administration. He knew that at stake was five-sevenths of the earth's surface, a vast, largely unknown area that suddenly could become the prize of a great power struggle.

The strident voices of sea power have already been raised. A Soviet scientist said recently, "The nation that first learns to live under the seas will control the world." And a distinguished American oceanographer said: "The capability of occupying a piece of the deep-sea bed would . . . make the placement of colonies on Antarctica, or even the moon, pale by comparison."

In late May 1968, the United States handed 46 other interested nations a "white paper" proposing an international decade of ocean exploration. The idea was first broached by President Johnson in March 1968 and had its roots in the recent technological breakthroughs that had been made in the marine sciences. It was hoped that the United States could take over the leadership of advancing the science of the seas, while the United Nations sought parallel solutions to the concurrent legal problems by committing itself to spend up to $5 billion during the next ten years.

Under the American plan, all sorts of far-out as well as immediately practicable projects would be undertaken, including both unmanned and manned operations. These would range from surface observations to expensive, submerged living complexes where men would have an opportunity to perfect new methods of exploiting the riches beneath the sea.

One of the more interesting projects for establishing stations on the ocean bottom was the recent announcement made by the Navy, the Space Agency, and the Department of the Interior that they would test a submerged, twin-chambered, research laboratory at a depth of 50 feet in the clear waters off St. John Island in the Virgin Islands. Called "Operation Tektite," the plan envisioned placing four American scientists, living and working for 60 consecutive days on the ocean floor, beginning in February 1969.

While space scientists have successfully mapped both the near-side and the hidden far-side of the moon, some 240,000 miles from earth, their counterpart marine scientists have been able to map a mere five percent of the ocean bottom, despite the fact that no known point on earth lies more than seven miles beneath the surface of the ocean. The time has come when man can no longer afford the luxury of ignorance concerning the ocean bottom. It is now generally conceded that marine farming and mining will probably be essential to feed and supply a burgeoning world population. As deposits of oil, gas and valuable minerals lying under dry land are depleted, the virtually untapped resources lying on and beneath the ocean floor become increasingly attractive to industry and the Government. In a 2,500,-000-square-mile offshore area covering a small portion of the Atlantic, Pacific, and the Gulf of Mexico, the United States has petroleum reserves estimated at 3.2 trillion barrels.

The expanding science of oceanology, which has relied so heavily on instrumented underseas probes from surface ships, has recently increased its demand for more manned exploration of the ocean depths. Spurred on by the need for effective submarine rescue-craft and anti-sub-

*This $9,300,000 floating laboratory, containing valuable, sophisticated, scientific equipment, became the new queen of the 14 research ships of the Coast and Geodetic Survey. With her sister-ship, the *Discoverer,* the United States was able to double her civilian oceanographic research capacity.

marine warfare systems, the U.S. Naval Oceanographic Office has been financing and encouraging the development of a number of devices that enable men to experiment and work far beneath the waves, at depths where the water pressure would crush conventional submarines.

This rising interest in the potential of the seas has spawned some bizarre and new deep-diving oceanographic research vessels. The Reynolds Metals Company's 51-foot-long *Aluminaut,* whose two 9-foot arms enable it to pick up samples of ore 3,000 feet beneath the surface, has already carried out surveys of potential manganese deposits off the Florida coast. The Perry-Link *Deep Diver,* an 8-ton submersible, can operate at a depth of 1,350 feet for up to 12 hours and allows divers to enter and leave the craft at will through an escape hatch. *Deepstar 4000,* the first of a family of Westinghouse underseas vehicles, is manned by a crew of three and can retrieve small objects from depths up to 4,000 feet. Lockheed's 40-foot-long, 50-ton *Deep Quest,* the most sophisticated of the new submersibles, can operate at an 8,000-foot depth with a crew of four. General Dynamics and General Motors have also entered the field of underwater research vehicles with sleek, manipulator-equipped craft.

More complex submersibles for oceanographic research are on their way. Lockheed's Deep Submergence Rescue Vehicle (DSRV) is one concept that can operate at depths of 20,000 feet and is equipped with a pressure chamber large enough to handle four divers. The DSRV can be flown to the site of distressed submarines or other research submersibles where it can descend and mate with an escape hatch on the sub, allowing the stranded crew to come aboard.

Encouraged by the performance of the foregoing submersibles, the Navy has recently ordered the first nuclear-powered research submersible, the NR-1. This new craft, being built by General Dynamics, will be able to sustain a crew of seven men under water for at least 30 days. It will be independent of surface support and will operate at "very great" (classified) depths. This sophisticated vessel, designed for convenient underwater pickup and discharge of divers, will contain the most advanced sensory and ocean-scanning devices known, and will even have outside electrical outlets, enabling divers to use insulated power tools in performing their tasks on the ocean bottom.

This vessel and the others represent another long step toward the eventual day when man will be able to live and work on the ocean floor with the aid of artificial gills. It will help to fufill a dream of Herman Melville who wrote: "There is, one knows not what sweet mystery about this sea, whose gently awful stirrings seem to speak of some hidden soul beneath."

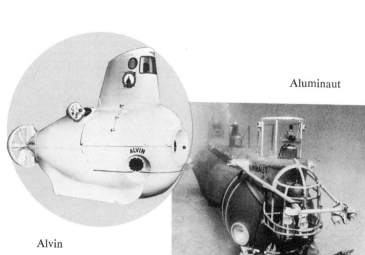

Aluminaut

Deepstar

Alvin

Further Reading

Bascom, Willard, *A Hole in the Bottom of the Sea*. Doubleday & Co., Inc., New York, 1961.

Bass, George, *Archaeology Under Water*. Frederick Praeger, New York, 1966.

Beebe, William, *Half Mile Down*. Duell, Sloan & Pearce, New York, 1951.

Carson, Rachel, *The Sea Around Us,* Oxford Univ. Press, New York, 1961.

Cousteau, Jacques-Yves, and Dumas, F., *The Silent World*. Harper and Brothers, New York, 1953.

Cowen, Robert, *Frontiers of the Sea.* Doubleday & Co., Inc., New York, 1960.

Daugherty, Charles, *Searchers of the Sea.* Viking Press, New York, 1961.

Deacon, G., ed., *Seas, Maps and Men.* Doubleday & Co., Inc., New York, 1962.

Douglas, John, *The Story of the Oceans.* Dodd, Mead & Co., New York, 1952.

Dugan, James, *Man Under the Sea.* Harper and Brothers, New York, 1956.

Engel, Leonard, *The Sea.* (Life Nature Library) Time Inc., New York, 1961.

Ericson, David, and Wollin, Goesta, *The Ever-Changing Sea,* Alfred A. Knopf, Inc., New York, 1967.

Guberlet, Muriel, *Explorers of the Sea.* Ronald Press, New York, 1964.

Hull, Seabrook, *The Bountiful Sea.* Prentice-Hall, New York, 1964.

Morris, Richard K., *John P. Holland.* U.S. Naval Institute, Annapolis, 1966.

Piccard, Jacques, and Dietz, Robert S., *Seven Miles Down.* G. P. Putnam's Sons, New York, 1961.

Raitt, Helen, *Exploring the Deep Pacific.* W. W. Norton & Company, Inc., New York, 1956.

Stewart, Harris, *The Global Sea.* D. Van Nostrand Co., Inc., Princeton, 1964.

Williams, Frances, *Matthew Fontaine Maury, Scientist of the Sea.* Rutgers University Press, New Brunswick, 1962.

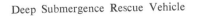

Deep Quest

Deep Submergence Rescue Vehicle

Index

Credits

Front endpaper: Gaylord Welker and Dwight Dobbins.   8,9: American Education Publications.   13: The Franklin Institute.   20: U.S. Navy.   21: Nicholas Zarrelli.   25: American Education Publications.   30: Martin A. Bacheller.   31,41,45: U.S. Navy.   54: American Education Publications.   59: Franklyn Hansen.   69: Ocean Systems, Inc.   88: U.S. Navy. 90: U.S. Navy, Reynolds Metals Company, Westinghouse Electric Corporation.   91: Lockheed Missile and Space Company. Back endpaper: Ernst Hofmann.

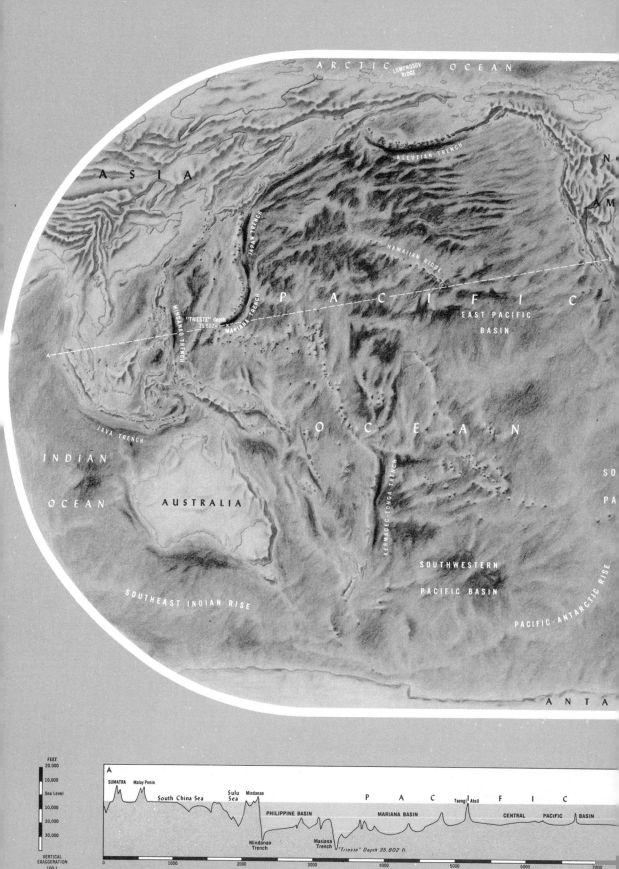

ARCTIC OCEAN

LOMONOSOV RIDGE

ALEUTIAN TRENCH

ASIA

N.
AM

PACIFIC

JAPAN TRENCH

HAWAIIAN RIDGE

B

MARIANA TRENCH

"TRIESTE" depth
35,802 — X

EAST PACIFIC
BASIN

MINDANAO TRENCH

MARIANA TRENCH

A

OCEAN

JAVA TRENCH

INDIAN

OCEAN

AUSTRALIA

KERMADEC-TONGA TRENCH

SO
PA

SOUTHWESTERN

PACIFIC BASIN

SOUTHEAST INDIAN RISE

PACIFIC-ANTARCTIC RISE

ANTA

FEET
20,000

10,000

Sea Level

10,000

20,000

30,000

VERTICAL
EXAGGERATION
100:1

A

SUMATRA   Malay Penin.

South China Sea

Sulu
Sea

Mindanao

P   A   C   I   F   I   C

Taongi Atoll

PHILIPPINE BASIN

MARIANA BASIN

CENTRAL   PACIFIC   BASIN

Mindanao
Trench

Mariana
Trench

"Trieste" Depth 35,802 ft.

0   1000   2000   3000   4000   5000   6000   7000

PROFILE   OF   THE   PACIFIC   OC